The Art of Brewing

by David Booth

with an introduction by Roger Chambers

Self Reliance Books

Get more historic titles on animal and stock breeding, gardening and old fashioned skills by visiting us at:

http://selfreliancebooks.blogspot.com/

Introduction

I am pleased to present yet another title on Brewing and Winemaking.

This volume is entitled "The Art of Brewing" and was published in 1829.

The work is in the Public Domain and is re-printed here in accordance with Federal Laws.

As with all reprinted books of this age that are intended to perfectly reproduce the original edition, considerable pains and effort had to be undertaken to correct fading and sometimes outright damage to existing proofs of this title. At times, this task is quite monumental, requiring an almost total "rebuilding" of some pages from digital proofs of multiple copies. Despite this, imperfections still sometimes exist in the final proof and may detract from the visual appearance of the text.

I hope you enjoy reading this book as much as I enjoyed making it available to readers again.

Roger Chambers

THE ART OF BREWING.

CHAPTER I.

Introductory.

THE artificial formation of exhilarating and intoxicating liquors has been practised in most ages and nations. Wine, which is prepared from the juice of the grape, is mentioned in the earliest records of history. The Tartar tribes, from time immemorial, manufactured their *kumis* from the milk of the mare and of the cow : the *chiaca* of the East Indies is the produce of rice : the Mexicans, before the arrival of the Spaniards, had different kinds of cheering liquors; from the *metl*, or *magnai*, a species of aloe (*Agave Mexicana*) ; from certain palms and from maize : and the Germans, in the time of Tacitus, brewed *zythum* and *curmi* from barley, in the manner in which we make our ALE and BEER.

All these preparations, and numerous others which we have not named, have certain properties in common. They constitute a genus, under the denomination of *Vinous Liquors*, because that of the vine is pre-eminent. They all acquire their inebriating quality from a similar fermentation ; and all give out fluids by distillation, in which that quality is concentrated in a far less bulk. These latter fluids are called, generally, *Spirits*, or *Spirituous Liquors ;* and have the specific names, *Brandy*, *Ariki*, *Arrack*, *Whisky*, &c. each differing from the others in flavour, according to the material from which it is drawn. They are all, however, convertible, by subsequent distillation, into the same sort of liquid, which is termed *Spirit of Wine*, or *Alcohol*. There are thus three stages or three processes : the fermentation which produces wine, beer, &c.; the distillation of these fermented liquors, producing spirits ; and the distillation of spirit, producing alcohol.

Although we were able, it is not our present business to describe the various processes by which vinous liquors may be prepared from different substances. What we here undertake is to treat of the Vinification of Barley ; and, when we shall have, occasionally, to speak of the fermentation of other vegetables, it will be solely for the purpose of eluci-dation. The comparison of Ale with Wine will be frequent ; but for the particular processes, by which the latter and its numerous imitations are produced and preserved, we must refer to the TREATISE ON WINE-MAKING.

Though Brewing is certainly a chemical art, it has hitherto derived little, if any, advantage from the science of chemistry. In fact, nothing is to be expected from that quarter. Of all material substances, vegetables are the most difficult to analyze. Their *immediate materials* (as the results are termed) are often *produced*, rather than *found*, in the laboratory. The acids are connected by an invisible chain. The *fecula*, or *starch*, becomes *gum*, or *sugar*, by almost imperceptible processes. The seeds of plants are endowed with a vegetable life, which is absolutely necessary to vinous fermentation. A vivifying power shall exist when the grain is cut to atoms, which an unlucky twist of the mill might have utterly destroyed. Our chemists are men of the closet ; and the manufacturer who operates on three hundred quarters of grain at a time can hope for little information from general theories, although upheld by the analyses of twenty barleycorns and their infusions in a quart bottle.

While the art of Brewing has been so little indebted to the progress of chemical knowledge, it has been considerably retarded by a power to which it had a right to look for assistance,—the Legislature of the country. The public Brewer, from whom only the art could receive improvement, is completely fettered by the laws of excise. The French *Vigneron* may flavour his wines at pleasure ; and, by means of extraneous substances, may prevent or cure their degenerations ; but malt, hops, water, and isinglass are the only materials of the British Brewer. Under whatever circumstances, everything else is inexorably prohibited. There is no distinction between useful and poisonous ingredients : all are stigmatized as illegal; and the penalty is the same for a single eggshell as for a pound of opium.

In addition to these absurd prohibitions, the public brewer has to struggle under a direct impost, amounting, in

B

most cases, to 50 per cent. on the first cost of his materials, and from which the private brewer is wholly free. The duties upon ale and beer brewed for sale, which were first imposed in 1643, have been increased, from time to time, until they have reached their present enormous amount. We shall not stop to trace their progress, but we may remark that, at a certain period, in distinguishing between small beer and strong, all ale or beer, sold at or above ten shillings per barrel, was reckoned to be *strong*, and was, therefore, subjected to a higher duty. The cask which contained this strong beer was then first marked with an X, signifying *ten;* and hence the present quack-like denominations of XX (double X), and XXX (treble X), which appear, unnecessarily, on the casks and in the accounts of the strong-ale brewers. A curious change of circumstances has rendered this letter still an appropriate mark in the books of excise. Ten shillings has no longer any relation to the *selling price*, but it is now the *duty* per barrel.

But it is not of the amount alone, but of the proportions in which the duty is levied, that the brewers, as well as their customers, have occasion to complain. Small beer is charged only at the rate of two shillings the barrel; and by small beer is understood all ale or beer that is sold to the customer at, or under, the price of twenty-four shillings. All that is sold above this price is accounted strong, and is liable to the ten shillings duty. The strength of the beer, which ought to be the criterion, is here out of the question; for, if any gentleman were to go to his ale brewer, and say that he wanted an article better than small beer, for which he would pay eight or ten shillings more, the brewer could not furnish it, because, if he charged more than twenty-four shillings per barrel, he would have to pay the ten shillings duty, so that he could not give a better article for thirty-two shillings a barrel than for twenty-four. A cheap table ale is nevertheless much in demand, and is often furnished at forty shillings, or less. The temptation to evade the strong ale duty is great, and, consequently, as appears from the numerous convictions, the mixing of strong beer with small beer is not uncommon. Were the duty, by some means, proportioned to the strength, this would seldom be done. But we should write a volume were we to detail all the frauds and inconveniences consequent upon the absurdities of the present brewery laws. In small works, unless the brewer will consent to adopt the measures of those whose consciences are not too confined, he will seldom succeed in his business.

It may be thought that we have dwelt too long on this subject, but we shall have frequent occasions to show that the laws of excise must undergo some change before the art of brewing can be much advanced, without involving the trade in total ruin. It is now preserved in consequence of the ignorance, or the indolence, of the servants in private families. The tax on public brewers is beyond all ordinary bounds. Were a penny a quartern loaf levied upon the bakers, their ovens would soon be cold; and yet we consent to pay *twopence* upon every pot of porter which we drink. In proof, the following is a statement of the expense at which any private gentleman, who understands the manipulations, might brew porter of as good a quality as any that is usually sold in London :—

	Shillings.
1 Quarter of Malt, at 65*s.* per quar. =	65
3 Quarters of Barley, at 40*s.* per quar. =	120
32 lbs. of Hops, at 112*s.* per cwt. =	32
Colouring, either from patent Malt or burnt Sugar . . }	5
Cost of Materials . .	222

To this there is nothing to add but the labour which, to those who keep men-servants, costs nothing. The grains and yeast may be considered as an indemnification for the coals. If the brewing were properly managed, it would produce fifteen barrels of porter, of the average London strength, at a price under *fifteen shillings* a barrel, or *five farthings* a pot. This calculation was made in 1827, and the value would, of course, vary with the alteration of prices, but the sketch here given is sufficient to prove that, under the present laws, were the art of brewing generally understood, the trade of a public brewer could exist only upon the earnings of the poor; for all who could muster a few pounds would brew for themselves. We have supposed *raw grain*, not so much on account of the saving of malt-duty as of its making a *better* beverage; but even were the porter made wholly of malt the saving would be enormous. Thus :

	Shillings.
4 Quarters of Malt, at 65*s.* per quar. =	260
32 lbs. of Hops, at 112*s.* per cwt.	32
Colouring	5

These materials would produce fifteen barrels of good porter, at less than 30s. per barrel, which is little more than three-halfpence the pot.

CHAPTER II.

Of Brewing Utensils.

ALTHOUGH the names and general use of the principal brewing utensils are almost universally known, yet a few remarks, upon their construction, may be of advantage to those who have not had experience in their erection.

§ 1.—Of Grinding Machines.

Malt is prepared for the mash-tun in two different ways,—by crushing, or by grinding. In the former case the malt is made to pass between two cylindric rollers, close enough to burst the skin and bruise the kernel. This answers the purpose very well with regard to good malt; but when we have occasion to make use of raw grain, or of grain that has not been sufficiently malted, there is a certain loss of materials which would be secured by grinding. The cause of this loss will appear afterwards, when we treat of the means of producing a saccharine extract.

Grinding is best performed by mill-stones cut sharp for the purpose. Private families cannot generally afford the expense of mill-stones, which, besides, are not now erected, like the querns of our ancestors, so as to be turned by a man. In the neighbourhood of corn-mills, the miller could do this duty; but his multure is seldom determinate. A steel-mill is the best succedaneum. It may be had of any size, and, consequently, at various prices, from three to ten guineas; and, we believe, there is no law to prevent a machine of this kind from serving a whole neighbourhood, unless it may be in special cases of thirlage.

By whatever machine the barley, or malt, is ground, it ought to be cut sharp and small; especially the former, which must on no account be powdered into dust, but cut into particles like sand or well-ground oatmeal; and, for this purpose, if not already hard, it must be dried on a kiln. Those who use small quantities may purchase the barley in that state, but licensed brewers, be it remembered, must not use it at all. The malt needs not to be ground so fine. Neither should it be kept above a day or two in a ground state, because all sorts of meal are apt to heat by reason of a fermentation that would terminate in putridity. We have known it clotted so hard that it required to be broken by a mallet; and the flavour, in consequence, was spoiled.

§ 2.—Liquor and Wort Coppers, and Underback.

Water, in the language of the brewhouse, is termed Liquor; the cut (or bruised) malt, or grain, is Grist; when put into the mash-tun it is called the Goods; and the extract made from these goods, by infusion in hot liquor, is termed Wort. The liquor-copper, then, is a boiler chiefly used in heating water, for the purpose of infusing the goods in the mash-tun, or for supplying any part of the brewhouse where hot water is required; and the wort-copper is that in which the worts are boiled, along with the hops, for the purpose of giving bitterness, flavour, and (as is generally believed) a preservative quality. In small works, and particularly in private families, one boiler is made to answer the double purpose of a liquor and a wort copper; but this is done always at some loss, and frequently at the risk of destruction to the whole brewing. When the FIRST MASH (or infusion) is ready to be drained, it must be drained into a vessel called an UNDERBACK, because the copper is not ready to receive it; being employed in heating liquor for the second mash. The same happens in the third and fourth mashes, if there are so many; and the wort, thus remaining so long in the underback, gradually becomes tepid, generally contracts a disagreeable flavour, and often turns into that peculiar state of acidity which the brewers designate by the denomination of BLINKED. This last evil, however, (which admits of no remedy) is sometimes occasioned by improper heats in the mash-tun; but there the accident is more easily guarded against, because it never occurs unless the heat of the mashing liquor has either been too low, or has been allowed to stand too long upon the goods. If the last runnings of the mash be free from any tincture of acidity, and if they can then be immediately carried to the copper and submitted to heat, the mishap of blinking will always be prevented; and this, by the assistance of two coppers, can be readily accomplished.

The expense of two coppers in place

of one may be urged as an objection; but the expense of one, on the ordinary construction, is often as much as both would be, if the coppersmith were properly directed. Coppers are generally made of twice or thrice the weight that is necessary. The sides can scarcely be too thin, and the bottom, if it will bear the weight of a man to stand while cleaning it, is of quite sufficient thickness. It should in all cases be well hammered and raised inwards, like the bottom of a wine-bottle; which not only strengthens it, but allows the worts to drain with more rapidity from the hops. In family coppers, the bottom can be scoured without any great pressure or weight.

Beside the saving in price, a thin-bottomed copper is much more easily heated, and less liable to wear, than a thick one. The inner surface of the bottom can never be hotter than the fluid which it contains: the outer surface is of course as hot as the flame which envelopes it. In a liquor copper, therefore, the inside can never exceed the heat of boiling water; and, if we could imagine a copper-bottom to be infinitely thin, the heat of the side next the fire would be absorbed, by passing through the copper as fast as it were generated. It is on this principle that water may be made to boil on a folded piece of writing-paper. On the other hand, when the bottom of the boiler is thick, the outer surface is submitted to the heat of the fire some time before it communicates with the liquor within. The metal becomes oxidated, and comes off in scales, or, if the scales remain, they render it more impervious to the heat, so as in some cases to take double the time of a thin bottom, before the liquor can be brought to the requisite heat. The difference of wear is an obvious consequence. We have ourselves made use of a twenty barrel liquor copper, which (the discharge cock included) did not weigh three hundred pounds, and we found it quite sound at the end of fifteen years, without having needed the slightest repair during all that period. The London allowance for a copper of that size would be eight or nine hundred weight.

With respect to the size of brewing-coppers, the liquor and wort coppers should be alike, and the contents of each must be regulated by the sort of beer to be brewed. If small beer alone, with three *mashes*, the first mash would require from three to four barrels of hot liquor per quarter of malt, according to the quality; and, as it is always convenient to have more liquor than is needed for the mash, so as to get the second mash liquor ready in time, he who would brew small beer in this way, ought to have a copper which would contain five barrels of liquor for every quarter of malt that he intends to brew at a time. Were he to brew strong ale, with small beer in succession, or porter alone, a copper containing about three barrels for every quarter of the mash would be a sufficient size. We are aware that many public, as well as private brewers, contrive to manage with a single copper, by means of pan-covers and other clumsy shifts; but our business is to teach the most convenient (which will always be found the most profitable) method of conducting the operation.

§ 3.—Of the Furnace.

Although the construction of the fire-place and other building (*setting*) of the copper is usually entrusted to the brick-layer, yet a well-going furnace is of such importance to the brewer, that we cannot pass over it in silence. In most manufactories, an ill-built fireplace is merely the cause of additional destruction of fuel, and unnecessary delay; but, in the brewery, the consequence is often more serious. If, for example, the second mashing liquor cannot be raised to the proper heat within a few minutes of a given time, the whole brewing of the day is in imminent danger of being lost. We shall, therefore, describe our method of *setting* a copper, the utility of which we have experienced for many years. It has the double advantage of being cheap, and, at the same time, equally applicable to coppers of any size.

There are a few general remarks which apply to every plan of *setting*. The furnace-bars, or grating on which the fuel is burnt, should bear a fixed proportion to the lower surface of the copper on which the heat is expended; but in this respect the artists do not materially differ. The same may be said of the height between the furnace-bars and the bottom of the vessel, which can scarcely be less than twelve, or more than eighteen, inches. The ash-pit should be as wide as the furnace-bars, and may descend as low as we please. Allowing the furnace-bars to be an inch and a half wide, and half an inch asunder, the air will be admitted, to supply the fire, through an area equal to one-fourth of the area of the fireplace. This air has to pass into the chimney, in an expanded form, accompanied with the smoke and vapour of the fuel, and in that state will occupy about double its former bulk. The chimney ought, therefore, to have a sectional area equal to half that of the fireplace; and, if so, it will only be the want of height in the chimney that can prevent a proper draught. These things being premised,

Let A B E C D (*fig.* 1.) be a flat piece of masonry, or brickwork, level with the furnace bars G F, and raised from the floor to the height of the ash-pit, which is immediately below the bars, and where only the building is not solid. Draw the dotted circle G H I K, exactly equal in size to the bottom of the copper. Opposite to the middle of the furnace G F erect the prop I, and at H and K, two other props, raising all three to the height at which you mean to fix your boiler above that of the furnace-bars.

Fig. 1.

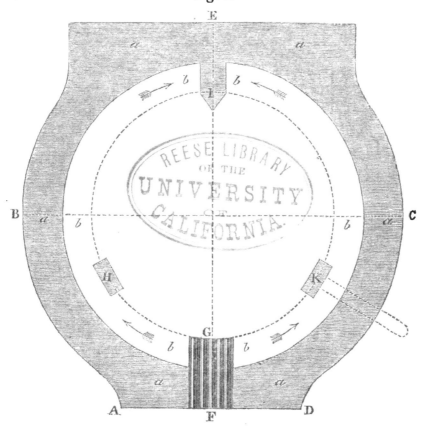

Place the rim of the bottom of the copper upon these props, which, as proper supports, must be built of fire-brick or of fire-stone. If the copper be very large, intermediate props may be built (always in the dotted circle), so as to support it for a time, were one of them to give way.

Let the surrounding part of the building a, a, a, &c. be carried upwards, higher than the bottom of the copper, by ten, twelve, fifteen, or any number of inches at pleasure, leaving a vacuity b, b, b, &c. around the copper to the height thus fixed upon, when it is to be covered at top by means of bricks leaning from the wall a, a, a, &c., to the

sides of the copper, the aperture not requiring a greater width at that height than the length of a brick: nor, indeed, in any place, need the aperture be more than from nine to twelve inches wide, unless the boiler be very large, in which case it may be covered by an arch. The prop I, should be continued across this vacuity, and raised so as the flame, when it has reached the roof of the aperture, shall just have sufficient room to pass easily over on both sides, into the chimney c, d, e, f, as represented at *fig.* 3, in which the prop I is marked on a section by the same letter I. By keeping the entry to the chimney at this height, the whole exposed part of the copper will be wrapped in flame; for it should always be kept in mind that the flame will rise as high and no higher than the opening by which it is allowed to enter the chimney.

Fig. 2 is a vertical section on the same scale, with the copper in its place.

Fig. 2.

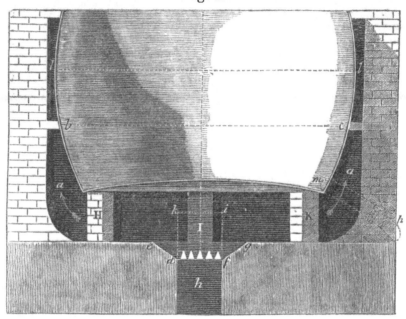

The lower part of this copper, being in the form of a truncated cone, allows the bottom (literally so called) to be smaller, and consequently lighter, than if the vessel had been cylindrical; while the flame, mounting up the sides at *a, a,* gives the same heating power, as if the bottom had been of a diameter equal to the line *b c.* After the circular vacuity is closed at *b* and *c,* the building round the copper (until again closed at the top) should be kept three or four inches from the sides, as represented at *l l*; and this thin zone of air will prevent the escape of the radiant heat, more effectually than would be done by two feet of solid masonry. The sides of the furnace are sloped to keep the fuel upon the bars, as in the lines *d e* and *f g.* This section is presumed to be made at the inner end of the furnace, where the ash-hole *h* ends. The place of the furnace door (which is cut off in front) is represented by the dotted rectangle *d, f, i, k.* The lighter shade I, seen behind this rectangle, is the prop I mentioned at (*fig.* 1.) The other two props H and K, are here also shown by the same letters.

Fig. 3 is another section of the copper and its building, through the line E F on the plan *fig.* 1. F is a section of the furnace; I is a central section of the prop I so often mentioned; and K is the prop K of *fig.* 1., the other prop being supposed to be cut away. The dark shade *a* is part of the open space which surrounds the lower part of the copper; and *b* is a portion of the same open space, the rest being covered by the prop I, over which prop, and on both sides of it, the flame ascends to *b,* entering the chimney *c d e f* at *c.* The dark narrow spaces *l l,* represent the same zone which was explained in *fig.* 2.

It will be observed, that the discharge pipe, *m n,* has to pass through the flame; it must, consequently, be a simple copper tube, riveted to the boiler, and joined to the cock, *p,* by a *flange* at *n.* This will, however, in a twenty-barrel copper, save a hundred weight, at least, of lead, which the coppersmiths usually pour into a socket, when joining a cock to a boiler, and which is weighed to the purchaser as copper. To be sure, were it not for this base metal, as well as the excessive weight of the whole, the coppersmith would be obliged to charge more per lb. for his labour. We do not mention these things as frauds, but as absurdities.

It would be out of our way to dwell long upon the erection of furnaces, and, therefore, we have left many of the details unnoticed. For our own part, we

Fig. 3.

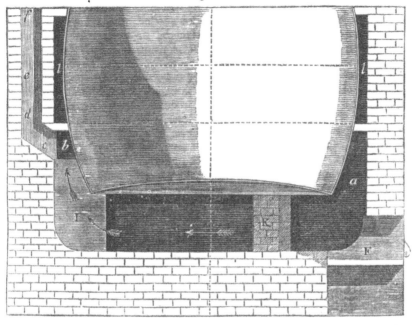

have generally found *ash-pit doors* and *upper dampers* more troublesome than useful—especially the latter—which are seldom so tight as to prevent a stream of cold air from entering the chimney, and thus disturbing the draught. We must not, however, neglect to mention what we have found from experience to be a great improvement in furnace-doors. These are often extremely troublesome. By their warping when thin, and shaking the building when weighty, they are perpetual sources of vexation. The improvement we allude to is cheap and simple, and by it we get immediate access to the furnace, without having to shove the coals through a passage two feet deep, which is made solely to keep the door steady on its hinges. The iron frame in front of the furnace is, in this case which we recommend, like that of the ordinary door-way, except that it is quite flat, (without any projection for latch or hinge,) and has a horizontal plate, about three inches broad, on a level with the bars, on which the substitute for a door is to rest. This door is a square, or rectangular fire-brick, (what is termed a Welsh tile,) about two inches thick, and of sufficient size to cover the opening of the fire-place, and an inch or two more on each side and at top, as far as the front-plate will allow. This tile is surrounded by a well-fitted hoop of iron, which, by means of a screw on one side, presses the other sides together so as to keep the tile firm. On the middle of the upper side

of the hoop is a staple, by which it is attached to a light iron chain, and the tile is so balanced, that when suspended the sides hang perpendicular. The chain is then passed over a pulley, so as the tile may drop directly before the fire-place, upon the plate above mentioned; when a weight exactly counterbalancing the tile is attached to the other end, so that this door may be raised, or lowered, at pleasure, with a very slight effort. By means of two or more pulleys, the countervailing weight may, like a bell-pull, be sent to any corner of the brew-house.*

CHAPTER III.

Of Brewing Utensils (continued).

§ 1.—*Of the Mash-Tun.*

SIMPLE as it still is, the mash-tun of former times was yet simpler than now. It was a tub with a hole in its centre, which was plugged by means of a round shaft of wood that stood perpendicularly through the goods. When the mash was to be drawn off, this shaft, which was called the *Tap-tree*, was loosened (but not altogether pulled out) from the hole, which, being *conical*, allowed the worts to descend in a small stream into the underback; and the filtration was assisted by a wisp of straw that had previously been wound about the *tap-*

* We are indebted for our knowledge of this useful contrivance to the late Mr. Parkes, who has described it in his " Chemical Essays, Vol. II."

tree, close to that part which acted as a plug to the tun. It is hence that the brewers still use the phrases of *setting-tap* in the sense of beginning to let off the worts from the *goods;* and *tap-spending*, or *tap-spent*, to announce that the goods are draining, or drained. Instead of this rude instrument, a *false bottom*, pierced with holes, is universally used; and the liquor, which was formerly poured upon the top of the malt, is now, in most cases, carried down the inside of the mash-tun, by a trough, and made to enter between the two bottoms, whence, rising upwards through the holes of the false bottom, it forces its way among the *goods*, with which it is then intimately mixed by the *mashing-machine*, or with *mashing-oars*.

The size of the mash-tun must be regulated by the quantity of malt and the quality of the beer for which it is to be employed. From this may be calculated the largest space that will require to be occupied by the goods and liquor of the mash; after which, five or six inches additional depth must be allowed, to leave room for the agitation when mashing. The liquor between the bottoms is not effective, and should, therefore, be as little as possible, consistent with the prevention of the risk of choking, with any deposite that might fall from the goods. An inch between the bottoms will be quite sufficient; in small areas, less. The holes of the false bottom should be burnt rather than bored, lest the pores of the wood should collapse with the hot liquor, which might put the first brewing in danger. To prevent this risk, by making wider holes, would be still worse: the holes should be conical; the lower part from a quarter to three-eighths of an inch diameter; but at the upper surface they ought not to exceed an eighth; the bottom should fit the sides of the mash-tun, and its parts should meet so as not to leave a chink.

We must advertise the private brewer, that, if he brew with a mixture of raw grain, it may sometimes happen that the goods in the first mash will sink to the lower part of the mash-tun and leave the wort floating above, without being able to filtrate through the condensed mass. To prepare for this contingency, the upper part of the trough that passes down the inner circumference of the tun and leads to the space between the bottoms, should be pierced with holes in the same manner as the false bottom. These holes, when not needed, may be shut by an interior trough, or by boards; and, when there is occasion to let off the worts from the top of the mash, the interior trough, or boards, may be pushed downwards, and the supernatant worts will pass through the holes, down the trunk, and, communicating with the space between the bottoms, may be drawn off in the same manner as if they had filtrated through the goods. With the second mash, this process will seldom, if ever, be necessary. In these observations we have supposed the mash-tun trough to be a close tube, but some give it only three sides, trusting to the inner surface of the tun (to which it is applied) for the fourth.

§ 2.—*Of Mashing Machines.*

Concerning mashing machines, we have very few observations to make. In large works they save much of human labour; but we should imagine that, until the mash extends to twenty quarters, they produce very little saving, unless under peculiar circumstances; such as the advantage of a waterfall, where the power costs nothing. In small works, and in private families, it is wholly out of the question. Oars are there the cheapest and the best mashing instruments.

§ 3.—*Of the Hop-back.*

After the wort is sufficiently boiled, along with the hops, it has to be carried into the coolers. If an airy situation can be had for this purpose, below the level of the discharge-cock of the wort-copper, the wort may be run off into the cooling-backs, either by means of a pipe or an open shoot, and the hops separated by means of a drainer in a corner of the first cooler, or *back* as it is termed by the excise; but when they cannot be cooled except at a higher elevation, the worts must be carried thither, either by hand, or by means of a pump. This pump may be placed directly into the copper; but, in that case, if the hops be in a great proportion, they will need to be inclosed in a net to prevent any accident from the choking of the valves. The ordinary way is to empty the copper into a hop-back, either round or square, on the upper part of which is fixed a drainer, (a perforated smaller vessel,) to keep back the hops. The pump is placed in the hop-back, and from thence raises the wort to the coolers. This wort-pump must differ from the common suction pump, if we expect *immediate* action. The lower valve must be placed at, or near, the bottom of the back; for that of the piston rod must be immersed in the fluid, as long as it gives out steam, before the action of the pump will be free. The valves, too, should be of metal, to resist the heat.

§ 4.—*Of the Coolers.*

It is of importance that the worts when drawn from the copper should be cooled, as speedily as possible, to that degree which fits them for the fermenting tun. This is more especially necessary in summer, and, therefore, the cooling back should be placed in that quarter where there is the best succession of fresh air; and the worts, if it can at all be prevented, ought never to lie above two inches deep in the coolers. This should regulate their size. The word *Coolers* is used in the plural, because two of these are indispensable when we make two kinds of beer from the same brewing; and even in single *Gyles*, if we make a *Return*. The two latter terms will be afterwards explained. One cooler ought to be placed so as to run into the other; and this, when we have occasion to speak of it, we shall call the *first* cooler,—the other the *second*. Sometimes three, or even four coolers are used, but these are more for conveniency than necessity.

Various contrivances have been proposed, and some of them adopted, for expediting the cooling of worts. That which is most commonly practised is the *fanning machine*, which is placed immediately above the cooler; and by the rapid revolution of its horizontal boards, or arms, produces a whirlpool of air which assists the ascent and dispersion of the steam. Whether or not this has any effect against the preservative quality of the beer, we are unable to determine. Reasoning *a priori* we should judge it to be unfavourable; but we have no support from experience. The *fanners* are employed only in the summer season, when beer for keeping is never brewed.

Another mode of cooling is to pass the worts through cold water, by means of a worm, in the manner of the distillers; but in that case the water would need to be plentifully supplied. Besides, it must be taken immediately from the spring, for that which is exposed for only a short time to the atmosphere, acquires its temperature, and gives no advantage over that of spreading the wort, in thin sheets, to the open air. Further—and we wish our observation to be applied to every attempt at improvement in his art—the public brewer ought to be very wary of introducing into his work any manipulation that is new. We knew a brewer whose situation was peculiarly adapted for the cooling method of which we speak. He practised it successfully for years, under the daily surveillance of the excise. Another superior officer at length came into the round. He found a clause, in an Act of Parliament, which made the process, in his view, *illegal*, although not *fraudulent*. The brewer was prosecuted in the Court of Exchequer. Instead of compromising the fault, he *foolishly* let it go to trial. He was *acquitted*, after his ingenuity had received an *eulogium* from the judges;—but *the Crown never pays expenses!*

The article *Brewing*, in the "Supplement to the Encyclopædia Britannica," (which was written by Dr. Thomson), contains the following remarks on the subject of which we now treat:—"When the brewer is obliged to make ale in warm summer weather, it is material to reduce the temperature as low as possible. In such cases, great advantage would attend cooling the worts in coolers without any roof, or covering whatever, but quite open to the sky; because, in clear nights, the wort might be cooled, in this way, eight or ten degrees lower than the temperature of the atmosphere. The reason is obvious. It is owing to the rays of heat which, in such a case, radiate from the wort, and are not returned again from the clear sky. Wort being a good radiator of heat, would be particularly benefited by this method of cooling." "A roof, perhaps, might be contrived, composed of very light materials, which might be easily slid off, or which might turn upon a pivot." "We have little doubt that wort might easily be cooled down to the freezing point, if requisite, in our warmest summer weather."

§ 5.—*Of the Fermenting Tuns.*

When the wort is considered as sufficiently cool, it is carried to the *Fermenting Tuns*, or the *Fermenting Squares*; some brewers using circular and others rectangular vessels for that purpose. The circular are, in our opinion, decidedly the best. Having no corners, they are more easily kept clean; and, in low fermentations, in the winter months, they are less liable to be chilled. The fermenting tuns are commonly termed *Gyle-tuns*, or *Working tuns*.

The size of the gyle-tun is regulated by the quantity of worts that have to be fermented within it at a time. It must, however, hold more than that quantity, to keep room for the head of yeast which rises during the progress. This head, if the vessel be cylindrical, is in proportion to the depth of the worts, without regard to the diameter of the tun. In certain modes of fermentation it may rise to a third, or even half of that depth. The number of tuns will depend on the more or less rapid succession of the brewings, and the time that they are suffered to remain before cleansing.

There are differing opinions with respect to using open or shut tuns, in the process of fermentation. Patents have been granted for particular applications of the latter mode, both in France and in this country, but of this we shall treat more appropriately when we have to investigate the nature and result of the operation in the *gyle-tun*.

§ 6.—*Of cleansing Casks, Stillions, and Store Vats.*

When the beer has received its assigned portion of fermentation in the tun, it is *cleansed*, that is, drawn off into other vessels. These are usually barrels, or other casks of a similar shape, in which the fermentation is finished by causing the yeast to be discharged from the bung-holes into *tubs*, or *stillions*, over which the barrels are placed. In order to keep up this purgation until all the yeast is wrought off, the *casks* are filled up, from time to time, with other beer. Some brewers take another mode, and finish the purgation in the tuns, by skimming off the yeast as it rises, after the fermentation has become languid. The comparative advantage of these modes will come again under our consideration. In porter - breweries, the beer, when it has ceased working, is usually turned into large close tuns termed *Store-vats*, in which it is mixed up with different brewings to suit the taste of the customers. Ale brewers, on the contrary, seldom rack their ale, but send it out in the casks where it received its final purgation. These practices, however, are in neither case universal. The reasons that determine these and other methods of cellarage,

in the minds of the several brewers, will afterwards appear.

§ 7.—*Of the Arrangement of the Plant.*

The general disposition of the *fixed utensils* (or *plant*) of a brewery must vary so much with the situation and extent of the building, that we can only give a general outline of the objects to be kept in view: leaving it to be filled up by the judgment of the engineer, or the ability of the proprietor.

If water cannot be had from a source sufficiently high, it should be raised to a *liquor-back* in quantity equal at least to one day's consumption, and high enough to command the whole work. Pipes, from this liquor-back, should be carried to every part of the brewery where they may be requisite. The liquor-copper should be the next in elevation, and from it, too, pipes should be carried. Immediately under, and as near as possible to the liquor-copper, we would place the *mash-tun* with a roomy stage, and, on the same floor, or a little higher, the *grinding machine*—at least that part of it where the ground malt called *grist* is given out. The mash tun should empty itself directly, by means of a pipe and cock, into the *wort-copper*; this again into the *hop-back*; and the hop-back, by means of a pipe or shoot, into the *first cooler*. The first cooler should run, if required, into the second, and both should communicate with a horizontal pipe running in front, and as low as the bottom of the gyle-tuns, (for these should be all on a level,) and communicating with each gyle-tun by stopcocks. From this horizontal pipe another should be carried to a contiguous cellar, below ground, which, by the assistance of screw-cocks and leather pipes, might cleanse any of the tuns into the casks. How much of all this can, in any particular case, be accomplished, we have here no means of determining. The plan of filling the gyle-tuns at the bottom instead of the top is not usual, but the young brewer will find it very commodious.

We are aware that many of the remarks and recommendations which we have hitherto given, will be considered as impracticable by private gentlemen, for whose use, as well as that of the public brewer, these pages are intended; but the accurate consideration of every subject has its use, and without this previous analysis we could scarcely hope to render the other parts of our work intelligible. The private brewer may have a more scanty store of utensils than those we have enumerated. They may even change their identity: his liquor-copper may become his wort-copper; his mash-tun may be metamorphosed into a gyle-tun; but he will understand what we mean, when we mention the different names, and will recognize the actors in their changes of character and dress.

CHAPTER IV.

Of Instruments.

§ 1.—*The Thermometer.*

BREWING is a philosophical art; and has gained advantages from some of those instruments which philosophy has invented. Few, if any, of the arts depend so much on the regulation of heat; and, notwithstanding, the introduction of the thermometer into the brewery was, we believe, not earlier than the middle of the last century. We are sure that then it was far from general; and even now it is unknown to nine-tenths of the private brewers. We are not, however, to judge from this circumstance, that our ancestors could not make good beer. They did so, but by no fixed rule. The guess-work often succeeded; and when, as was frequently the case, a brewing was *blinked* or otherwise spoiled, the blame was laid upon thunder, or upon witchcraft. Yet, even in those times, there were scientific brewers, who were able to do to-day what they did yesterday, though they could not communicate their knowledge. As is said of the blind,—the *other* senses became more acute from the want of artificial instruments; and the taste, touch, hearing, smell, and sight, were more forcibly put in requisition. We know a public brewer, still in business, in a country town, whose scientific acquirements are of the lowest rank, who exposes only the bottom of his copper to the fire, keeping the sides uncovered and polished; and who, nevertheless, fixes the heats of his mashing liquor, with surprising exactness, by the sound which his copper gives when beat with his KNUCKLES. With all this, he has little or no musical ear.

The thermometer is applicable and useful in every stage of the brewing process. It ascertains the heat of the mashing liquor, and of the worts when draining from the mash-tun. In the coolers, it shows when the worts are ready to let down for fermentation;

and in the gyle-tun it marks the progress, as far as it is notified by the increase or diminution of the heat. For the latter purpose there are tun-thermometers, from three to three and a-half feet long, which can be immersed in the worts, while all that is necessary of the scale overtops the froth of the head. An improved thermometer for the liquor-copper is still a *desideratum*. In high heats the steam covers the tube and obscures the mercury, so as easily to produce a mistake. We have often proposed, that a red glass bead should be introduced into the tube, which would swim on the top of the metallic fluid; but we have never been able to find an artist who would undertake to produce such an instrument, though it would certainly procure a ready sale. Perhaps a slight portion of coloured glass-dust might be inserted, so as to answer the purpose.

§ 2.—*The Saccharometer.*

The principle and construction of the *hydrometer* (or *areometer*) have been already explained in our "Treatise on Hydrostatics." The *saccharometer* is nothing else but a *hydrometer*, whose scale is calculated so as to render it peculiarly fitted for measuring the specific gravities of worts, as compared with water. The infusion of malt is *sweet*, and without stopping to investigate whether or not that sweet substance (which is extracted from the malt and increases the weight of the water) is homogeneous with the sugar (Latin *saccharum*) of the cane, the infusion is termed *saccharine*; the additional gravity which it exhibits beyond that of water is said to be caused by the *saccharine matter*, and is measured by the *saccharometer*.

The first instrument under the name of a *saccharometer* was constructed, and sold to the trade in 1784, by Mr. John Richardson, then a brewer at Hull. Other saccharometers have since appeared with various claims to superiority; but the fundamental principle of all is the same, and though Mr. Richardson's instrument has been *theoretically*, it has never been *practically*, improved. Extreme nicety is not necessary to the Brewer. What is wanted is a *cheap instrument*, which might be bought by private families; for we know of none at present that can be had under three guineas, except certain rudely-constructed glass ones, which have no pretensions to accuracy. We trust that we shall soon be able to supply this deficiency.

Mr. Richardson's saccharometer, if adapted to the imperial gallon, may be thus described:

The part A (*fig.* 4) is a hollow ball of copper, having a flat brass stem *c d*, and a weight *a* of the same metal affixed by the foot-stalk *g h*. The weight *a* is regulated so as the instrument shall sink in distilled water of 62º to the point *b* of the scale *e b*, which is divided into ten equal parts. A barrel (36 gallons) of pure water at 62º heat, weighs 360 pounds avoirdupois; and the instrument is so regulated that, if put into a liquid weighing 361 pounds per barrel, it would rise to the mark *e*. Each of the divisions between *e* and *b* will then represent tenths of a pound. There are weights (having holes in their centres) marked 1, 2, 3, 4, 5, 10, 20 and 30. These, respectively, represent pounds weight, and are put, as required, on the top of the stem, resting on the projection *d*. So, for example, if when putting on the weight marked 10, the instrument sinks in a wort to the point *b*, a barrel of that wort, at the heat above specified, would weigh exactly ten pounds more than a barrel of pure water. If the instrument shall cut the surface at two of the divisions below the point *b*, in that case a barrel of the liquid would weigh 10.2 lb. more than a barrel of water—that is, 370.2 pounds. The length of the instrument is about eight inches, to which the ball is proportioned, as in the figure. The worts are understood to be cooled down to a certain heat (in our description 62º), and an allowance is made at other heats, as directed, by a table which accompanies the instrument.

The water used by the Brewer is seldom or never pure, but is often a tenth, and sometimes a half of a pound weightier per barrel. This should be kept in mind in taking the gravities of the worts, or the instrument may be regulated to the water by shortening *a h*; the part *g* sliding into the socket *g h*.

The common hydrometers, instead of proportioning the specific gravities of fluids to 360 parts of water, as is here done, compare them with 1000 parts; as may be seen in the Table of Specific

Gravities, given in the Treatise on Hydrostatics. The principle, nevertheless, is the same. Sea-water, for example, in that table, is marked 1028, while distilled water is 1000: that is, the same measure of the latter which would weigh 1000 ounces, or pounds, would, if filled with sea-water, weigh 1028. If we wish to reduce the saccharometer indications to the proportion of a thousand, we have only to multiply them by $2\frac{7}{9}$, because 1000 is $2\frac{7}{9}$ times 360. Thus a wort which shows 9 lb. by the saccharometer is equal to 25 parts of 1000, and in the table of gravities would be written 1025. But the Brewer never adds the weight of the water when speaking of his worts. A wort, the barrel of which weighs 370 pounds, is merely called a ten pound wort, and in this way all his calculations are made.

For the convenience of those who wish to compare specific gravities generally, as they appear in philosophical works, we subjoin the following table. The figures of the left hand marginal column are understood to be pounds; and those of the upper horizontal line, tenths of a pound weight, per barrel, as indicated by the common saccharometer. The body of the table contains specific gravities, extending to tenths and corresponding with the different weights, water being reckoned 1000. An example or two will be sufficient to show the mode of consultation.

Suppose we have a wort of 14 lb., and wish to know its specific gravity. In the left-hand margin we find 14; and next to that in the adjoining column marked at top by a cypher, there being no tenths, we find 1038.9, the specific gravity required. Again, let the saccharometer-weight be 32.4 lb. Opposite to 32, in the margin, and in the same horizontal line, in the column headed .4, we have 1090, for the equivalent specific gravity; and thus that of any wort under 50 pounds weight may readily be found.

The reverse of this comparison is equally easy. Thus, suppose we have a wort which shows a specific gravity of 1109.5 by the common hydrometer; and we want to know how many pounds heavier a barrel of such worts is than a barrel of water: we seek, in the body of the table, for the nearest number to 1109.5, which we find to be 1109.4. This sum is in the column headed .4, in the horizontal line with the left-hand margin 39; and therefore 39.4 is the weight sought for.

Fig. 4.

TABLE FOR REDUCING POUNDS AND TENTHS OF ADDITIONAL GRAVITY PER BARREL INTO PARTS OF 1000.

lb	.0	.1	.2	.3	.4	.5	.6	.7	.8	.9
0	1000.0	1000.3	1000.6	1000.8	1001.1	1001.4	1001.7	1001.9	1002.2	1002.5
1	1002.8	1003.1	1003.3	1003.6	1003.9	1004.2	1004.4	1004.7	1005.0	1005.3
2	1005.6	1005.8	1006.1	1006.4	1006.7	1006.9	1007.2	1007.5	1007.8	1008.1
3	1008.3	1008.6	1008.9	1009.2	1009.4	1009.7	1010.0	1010.3	1010.6	1010.8
4	1011.1	1011.4	1011.7	1011.9	1012.2	1012.5	1012.8	1013.1	1013.3	1013.6
5	1013.9	1014.2	1014.4	1014.7	1015.0	1015.3	1015.6	1015.8	1016.1	1016.4
6	1016.7	1016.9	1017.2	1017.5	1017.8	1018.1	1018.3	1018.6	1018.9	1019.2
7	1019.4	1019.7	1020.0	1020.3	1020.6	1020.8	1021.1	1021.4	1021.7	1021.9
8	1022.2	1022.5	1022.8	1023.1	1023.3	1023.6	1023.9	1024.2	1024.4	1024.7
9	1025.0	1025.3	1025.6	1025.8	1026.1	1026.4	1026.7	1026.9	1027.2	1027.5
10	1027.8	1028.1	1028.3	1028.6	1028.9	1029.2	1029.4	1029.7	1030.0	1030.3
11	1030.6	1030.8	1031.1	1031.4	1031.7	1031.9	1032.2	1032.5	1032.8	1033.1
12	1033.3	1033.6	1033.9	1034.2	1034.4	1034.7	1035.0	1035.3	1035.6	1035.8
13	1036.1	1036.4	1036.7	1036.9	1037.2	1037.5	1037.8	1038.1	1038.3	1038.6
14	1038.9	1039.2	1039.4	1039.7	1040.0	1040.3	1040.6	1040.8	1041.1	1041.4
15	1041.7	1041.9	1042.2	1042.5	1042.8	1043.1	1043.3	1043.6	1043.9	1044.2
16	1044.4	1044.7	1045.0	1045.3	1045.6	1045.8	1046.1	1046.4	1046.7	1046.9
17	1047.2	1047.5	1047.8	1048.1	1048.3	1048.6	1048.9	1049.2	1049.4	1049.7
18	1050.0	1050.3	1050.6	1050.8	1051.1	1051.4	1051.7	1051.9	1052.2	1052.5
19	1052.8	1053.1	1053.3	1053.6	1053.9	1054.2	1054.4	1054.7	1055.0	1055.3
20	1055.6	1055.8	1056.1	1056.4	1056.7	1056.9	1057.2	1057.5	1057.8	1058.1
21	1058.3	1058.6	1058.9	1059.2	1059.4	1059.7	1060.0	1060.3	1060.6	1060.8
22	1061.1	1061.4	1061.7	1061.9	1062.2	1062.5	1062.8	1063.1	1063.3	1063.6
23	1063.9	1064.2	1064.4	1064.7	1065.0	1065.3	1065.6	1065.8	1066.1	1066.4
24	1066.7	1066.9	1067.2	1067.5	1067.8	1068.1	1068.3	1068.6	1068.9	1069.2
25	1069.4	1069.7	1070.0	1070.3	1070.6	1070.8	1071.1	1071.4	1071.7	1071.9
26	1072.2	1072.5	1072.8	1073.1	1073.3	1073.6	1073.9	1074.2	1074.4	1074.7
27	1075.0	1075.3	1075.6	1075.8	1076.1	1076.4	1076.7	1076.9	1077.2	1077.5
28	1077.8	1078.1	1078.3	1078.6	1078.9	1079.2	1079.4	1079.7	1080.0	1080.3
29	1080.6	1080.8	1081.1	1081.4	1081.7	1081.9	1082.2	1082.5	1082.8	1083.1
30	1083.3	1083.6	1083.9	1084.2	1084.4	1084.7	1085.0	1085.3	1085.6	1085.8
31	1086.1	1086.4	1086.7	1086.9	1087.2	1087.5	1087.8	1088.1	1088.3	1088.6
32	1088.9	1089.2	1089.4	1089.7	1090.0	1090.3	1090.6	1090.8	1091.1	1091.4
33	1091.7	1091.9	1092.2	1092.5	1092.8	1093.1	1093.3	1093.6	1093.9	1094.2
34	1094.4	1094.7	1095.0	1095.3	1095.6	1095.8	1096.1	1096.4	1096.7	1096.9
35	1097.2	1097.5	1097.8	1098.1	1098.3	1098.6	1098.9	1099.2	1099.4	1099.7
36	1100.0	1100.3	1100.6	1100.8	1101.1	1101.4	1101.7	1101.9	1102.2	1102.5
37	1102.8	1103.1	1103.3	1103.6	1103.9	1104.2	1104.4	1104.7	1105.0	1105.3
38	1105.6	1105.8	1106.1	1106.4	1106.7	1106.9	1107.2	1107.5	1107.8	1108.1
39	1108.3	1108.6	1108.9	1109.2	1109.4	1109.7	1110.0	1110.3	1110.6	1110.8
40	1111.1	1111.4	1111.7	1111.9	1112.2	1112.5	1112.8	1113.1	1113.3	1113.6
41	1113.9	1114.2	1114.4	1114.7	1115.0	1115.3	1115.6	1115.8	1116.1	1116.4
42	1116.7	1116.9	1117.2	1117.5	1117.8	1118.1	1118.3	1118.6	1118.9	1119.2
43	1119.4	1119.7	1120.0	1120.3	1120.6	1120.8	1121.1	1121.4	1121.7	1121.9
44	1122.2	1122.5	1122.8	1123.1	1123.3	1123.6	1123.9	1124.2	1124.4	1124.7
45	1125.0	1125.3	1125.6	1125.8	1126.1	1126.4	1126.7	1126.9	1127.2	1127.5
46	1127.8	1128.1	1128.3	1128.6	1128.9	1129.2	1129.4	1129.7	1130.0	1130.3
47	1130.6	1130.8	1131.1	1131.4	1131.7	1131.9	1132.2	1132.5	1132.8	1133.1
48	1133.3	1133.6	1133.9	1134.2	1134.4	1134.7	1135.0	1135.3	1135.6	1135.8
49	1136.1	1136.4	1136.7	1136.9	1137.2	1137.5	1137.8	1138.1	1138.3	1138.6

§ 3.—*Assay Jars.*

These are used for the purpose of holding the worts which are to be weighed by the saccharometer. Their number is not limited, and may be only one or half a dozen, if it be wished to keep samples of the several worts. They are cylindric vessels of common tinned iron, about eight inches long and two and a-half diameter, which size gives sufficient space to swim the saccharometer. They have each a small handle and a lid, as represented in *fig.* 5.

Fig. 5.

§ 4.—*Refrigerator.*

This is a very necessary article; for though the saccharometers are usually accompanied with tables of expansion to show the allowance for the heat above or below sixty degrees, yet the worts can never be properly weighed, on account of the steam, until they are brought down to 90 at most. This refrigerator is so well described by Mr. Richardson, that we cannot do better than give it in his own words:—

"This instrument may be made of tin, and being intended to contain no more than the quantity of an assay-jar full, its dimensions may be nine or ten inches deep, and its breadth seven inches one way, and half an inch the other, forming a broad and flat, or thin vessel, resembling a tin case, sometimes made use of for the preservation of deeds or other writings. (See *fig.* 6.) The rea-

son of its being made thus thin is, that when charged with hot wort, and plunged into cold water, the effect of the cold may be almost instantaneous, which is nearly the case; for the quantity of wort being less than a pint, and the surface brought into contact with the cold water (the intervention of the tin only excepted), containing about 140 square inches, it may easily be conceived how rapidly the heat must be dissipated.

"The upper part should have a lip *a* for the more conveniently pouring out the wort; and on the opposite side should be a socket, to which a handle, *b*, should be soldered. The use of the socket is to receive a stick, of any convenient length, *c*, which is to fix in the socket by a pin, in the same manner as a bayonet is fixed; by which means it may be fastened in, when the refrigerator is to be dipped

Fig. 6.

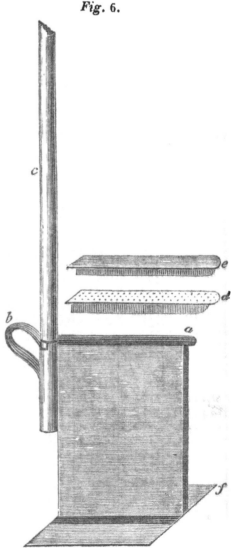

into the copper, and taken out, as an incumbrance, when it is charged with wort. It is to have two lids, or covers, *d* and *e*, the rims of which are to slip within the edge of the vessel, as is recommended for those of the assay-jars. One of the covers is to be perforated full of small holes, in order to admit the wort, and at the same time to prevent the hops from entering; the other is to be whole, and is intended to supply the place of the first the moment it is taken out of the copper.

"The length of the stick inserted in the socket is entirely to be determined by circumstances, it being intended only as the means of holding the refrigerator in the wort, till it is filled without endangering the hand from the steam.

"It should have a broad flat bottom, *f*, in order to enable it to stand upright, otherwise there would be a necessity of supporting it in that position."*

Chapter V.

Of Solutions and Mixtures.

§ 1.—Of Solutions.

WHEN a solid substance is dissolved in a liquid, the specific gravity of the compound is not increased by the whole weight of the solid dissolved. Part goes to the increase of bulk, and this increase differs with the nature of the bodies so united, in such a manner as not to be included under any general law that has been hitherto discovered. There is a marked distinction between mechanical and chemical union. A substance, for example, which has the same specific gravity as water would be suspended in that fluid, and, if reduced to dust, might be thoroughly mixed; but the mixture would be turbid, and the specific gravity of the water would remain the same. The suspended particles would increase the bulk exactly in proportion to the added weight. In chemical unions, however, (although we are pretty ignorant of their cause,) it is otherwise. In the mixture of fluids we are uncertain, previous to experiment, whether their volume will be increased or diminished. In certain proportions of alcohol and water, the diminution of bulk is about three per cent., and, as might be expected from theory, heat is produced. The solution, notwithstanding, remains transparent, without deposition. The

* "Richardson's Philosophical Principles of the Science of Brewing." 1798.

alcohol and the water are united, that neither is decomposed.

The manner in which the hot liquor absorbs the substance, termed saccharine, from the malt, has not been sufficiently observed. It would appear, from a few circumstances which have been noted, that there exists a condensation during the absorption, and that caloric is evolved; for the heat of the mash is often considerably above the mean of the ingredients. This, however, may be occasioned by the action of *Saccharification*, of which we shall afterwards have occasion to speak.

However all these things may be, it is certain that the weight of the dry substance extracted from the malt is much greater than that which is communicated to the specific gravity of the worts; for, if we were to take a barrel of worts which weighed 380 pounds, that is, twenty pounds more than water (as might be shown either by the saccharometer or by actual weighing); and were we to evaporate the water at a low heat until nothing remained but a dry residuum, that residuum would probably be found to weigh about fifty-two pounds: at least, this is nearly the result of experiments that have been made. The specific gravity of this residuum is stated by Dr. Thomson to be 1.532; but, we believe, he was never able to procure it in a solid form. At any rate, as we shall have afterwards to speak of the nature of malt extracts, we shall take our illustration of the present subject from the solution of sugar.

Pure sugar, dry and without vacuities, has a specific gravity of about 1.6, compared with water as unity; that is, a gallon measure of this sugar would weigh sixteen pounds, while water weighs only ten. If, then, we put one gallon measure of this solid sugar into thirty-five gallons of water, we shall (setting aside concentration, if there be any) have thirty-six gallons, or a barrel, of a solution, which will weigh sixteen pounds more than the water with which the sugar was mixed. If, instead of the gallon of sugar, we had put in another gallon of water to fill the barrel, we should then have added only ten pounds to the weight of the thirty-five gallons; so that we have a barrel, of sugar wort, which weighs six pounds more than a barrel of water will do; and these six pounds are all that are shown by the saccharometer. In the one case we have

35 gallons of water, at 10 lbs. per gallon   .   350 lb.
And   1 gallon of solid sugar, at 16 lb. per gallon   16
_____
Or 36 gallons of a solution weighing   . . .   366
In the other   36 gallons of water, weighing   360
_____
The difference of weight being   6 lbs.

A barrel, therefore, of a fluid mixture of sugar and water, which weighs six pounds more than a barrel of water, contains sixteen pounds of pure sugar; and this proportion of six to sixteen is found to prevail, with little variation, whatever be the quantity of sugar dissolved, as long as the fluidity is preserved. Thus a wort of 14 pounds would contain nearly $37\frac{1}{3}$ pounds of sugar; because 14 is to $37\frac{1}{3}$ in the ratio of 6 to 16.

When Mr. Richardson constructed his saccharometer, he was not aware of the distinction between the specific gravity of a wort and the quantity of *saccharum* which it contained. He mistook the one for the other, and uniformly spoke of a barrel of wort of ten, twenty, or any other number of pounds, as containing the same number of pounds' weight of fermentable matter. Further, however, than this misnomer, his instrument was accurately as well as ingeniously contrived; and we still consider it to be as well adapted to the brewery as any one that has succeeded it. Pounds and tenths of a pound per barrel are near enough for the purpose of the brewer, without having recourse to sliding rules, in the use of which he may be apt to err. Besides, this proportional specific gravity is accurately true and obvious to his understanding; whereas the *real* amount of fermentable matter, the discovery of which depends upon experiments that he cannot verify, is in every case an approximation or guess-work, rather than a certainty. The following Table will, at all events, enable him, if he wishes it, to turn his weights into *real fermentable matter*, according to the average of the scales of the more recent saccharometers. The method of consultation is the same as in the Table of specific gravities at page 13. The left-hand marginal column gives the pounds, and the upper horizontal line the tenths of a pound of gravity per barrel; and the body of the Table, in the squares to which the side and top figures respectively point, contain the corresponding qualities of dry saccharine matter, which those gravities are supposed to indicate, expressed also in pounds and decimals of a pound.

TABLE OF POUNDS OF FERMENTABLE MATTER CORRESPONDING TO THE POUNDS PER BARREL OF GRAVITY; AVERAGED FROM THE MODERN SACCHAROMETERS.

	0	.1	.2	.3	.4	.5	.6	.7	.8	.9
0		.25	.50	.76	1.01	1.26	1.51	1.76	2.02	2.27
1	2.52	2.77	3.02	3.28	3.53	3.78	4.03	4.28	4.54	4.79
2	5.04	5.29	5.54	5.80	6.05	6.30	6.55	6.80	7.06	7.31
3	7.56	7.81	8.06	8.32	8.57	8.84	9.09	9.32	9.58	9.83
4	10.08	10.33	10.58	10.84	11.09	11.34	11.59	11.84	12.10	12.35
5	12.60	12.85	13.10	13.36	13.61	13.86	14.11	14.36	14.62	14.87
6	15.12	15.37	15.62	15.88	16.13	16.38	16.63	16.88	17.14	17.39
7	17.64	17.89	18.14	18.40	18.65	18.90	19.15	19.40	19.66	19.91
8	20.16	20.41	20.66	20.92	21.17	21.42	21.67	21.92	22.18	22.43
9	22.68	22.93	23.18	23.44	23.69	23.94	24.19	24.44	24.70	24.95
10	25.20	25.45	25.70	25.96	26.21	26.46	26.71	26.96	27.22	27.47
11	27.72	27.97	28.22	28.48	28.73	28.98	29.23	29.48	29.74	29.99
12	30.24	30.49	30.74	31.00	31.25	31.50	31.75	32.00	32.26	32.51
13	32.76	33.01	33.26	33.52	33.77	34.02	34.27	34.52	34.78	35.03
14	35.28	35.53	35.78	36.04	36.29	36.54	36.79	37.04	37.30	37.55
15	37.80	38.05	38.30	38.56	38.81	39.06	39.31	39.56	39.82	40.07
16	40.32	40.57	40.82	41.08	41.33	41.58	41.83	42.08	42.34	42.59
17	42.84	43.09	43.34	43.60	43.85	44.10	44.35	44.60	44.86	45.11
18	45.36	45.61	45.86	46.12	46.37	46.62	46.87	47.12	47.38	47.63
19	47.88	48.13	48.38	48.64	48.89	49.14	49.39	49.64	49.90	50.15
20	50.40	50.65	50.90	51.16	51.41	51.66	51.91	52.16	52.42	52.67
21	52.92	53.17	53.42	53.68	53.93	54.18	54.43	54.68	54.94	55.19
22	55.44	55.69	55.94	56.20	56.45	56.70	56.95	57.20	57.46	57.71
23	57.96	58.21	58.46	58.72	58.97	59.22	59.47	59.72	59.98	60.23
24	60.48	60.73	60.98	61.24	61.49	61.74	61.99	62.24	62.50	62.75
25	63.00	63.25	63.50	63.76	64.01	64.26	64.51	64.76	65.02	65.27
26	65.52	65.77	66.02	66.28	66.53	66.78	67.03	67.28	67.54	67.79
27	68.04	68.29	68.54	68.80	69.05	69.30	69.55	69.80	70.06	70.31
28	70.56	70.81	71.06	71.32	71.57	71.82	72.07	72.32	72.58	72.83
29	73.08	73.33	73.58	73.84	74.09	74.34	74.59	74.84	75.10	75.35
30	75.60	75.85	76.10	76.36	76.61	76.86	77.11	77.36	77.62	77.87
31	78.12	78.37	78.62	78.88	79.13	79.38	79.63	79.88	80.14	80.39
32	80.64	80.89	81.14	81.40	81.65	81.90	82.15	82.40	82.66	82.91
33	83.16	83.41	83.66	83.92	84.17	84.42	84.67	84.92	85.18	85.43
34	85.68	85.93	86.18	86.44	86.69	86.94	87.19	87.44	87.70	87.95
35	88.20	88.45	88.70	88.96	89.21	89.46	89.71	89.96	90.22	90.47
36	90.72	90.97	91.22	91.48	91.73	91.98	92.23	92.48	92.74	92.99
37	93.24	93.49	93.74	94.00	94.25	94.50	94.75	95.00	95.26	95.51
38	95.76	96.01	96.26	96.52	96.77	97.02	97.27	97.52	97.78	98.03
39	98.28	98.53	98.78	99.04	99.29	99.54	99.79	100.04	100.30	100.55
40	100.80	101.05	101.30	101.56	101.81	102.06	102.31	102.56	102.82	103.07
41	103.32	103.57	103.82	104.08	104.33	104.58	104.83	105.08	105.34	105.59
42	105.84	106.09	106.34	106.60	106.85	107.10	107.35	107.60	107.86	108.11
43	108.36	108.61	108.86	109.12	109.37	109.62	109.87	110.12	110.38	110.63
44	110.88	111.13	111.38	111.64	111.89	112.14	112.39	112.64	112.90	113.15
45	113.40	113.65	113.90	114.16	114.41	114.66	114.91	115.16	115.42	115.67
46	115.92	116.17	116.42	116.68	116.93	117.18	117.43	117.68	117.94	118.19
47	118.44	118.69	118.94	117.20	119.45	119.70	119.95	120.20	120.46	120.71
48	120.96	121.21	121.46	119.72	121.97	122.22	122.47	122.72	122.98	123.23
49	123.48	123.73	123.98	122.24	124.49	124.74	124.99	125.24	125.50	125.75

C

§ 2.—*Mixture of Worts.*

The different extracts from malt, if properly taken, seem to be homogeneous. Whatever be their gravity they unite readily with each other, as well as with water, in all proportions; and the mixture is invariably a mean between two extracts with regard to specific gravity, and equal to both in quantity. This regularity in their union renders it an easy task for the brewer to increase, or diminish the gravity of his worts at pleasure; and, as far as strength is concerned, to fix the value of his beer. We shall here give a few examples of the manner of making up strengths; in order to save repetitions when we make our statements of different brewings:—When there is only one kind of beer made from the same goods (what is termed *Entire Gyles*) the mixture of worts requires no calculation. The strength is fixed by the union of the whole; and if that strength be too small there is no remedy but to boil longer, or to be more careful when we mash for another brewing. If the strength of the whole be too great, they may be brought down by letting water into the wort-copper; but this practice is clumsy, and wasteful: for something better might have been got from the goods by sprinkling, if done before the chance of acidity. It is when two qualities of beer (such as strong and small) are made from the same brewing, that the mixing of the worts requires particular calculation. It is to be premised, in the outset, that the brewer must have tables of the contents of his coppers and working tuns for every inch of their depth, and of the coolers for every tenth of an inch. In public breweries these tables are all drawn up by the excise, in barrels, firkins, and gallons; but it will be found more convenient by the brewer, if they are calculated in barrels and tenths, which is minute enough for the purpose which we have now in view to explain.

		Barrels.	lb. gravity.		
Suppose					
1st Wort		12	at 35	=	420
2d Wort		14	at 20	=	280
3d Wort		14	at 6	=	84
		40	at 19.6 av.	=	784

Here we have forty barrels of wort, which, if all mixed, would average 19.6 lbs. per barrel. This would be too weak for ale, and too strong for small beer. Let the worts, therefore, be mixed up in other proportions, such as the following:—

	Barrels.	lb. gravity.		
1st Wort	12	at 35	=	420
2d Wort	7	at 20	=	140
Strong Ale	19	at 29.4	=	560

There now remains of

	Barrels.	lb. gravity.		
2d Wort	7	at 20	=	140
3d Wort	14	at 6	=	84
Making	21	at 10.6	=	422

which would be saleable small beer. Should we wish it, we might improve the quality of both, in this, or some similar manner:—

	Barrels.	lb. gravity.		
1st Wort	12	at 35	=	420
2d Wort	2	at 20	=	40
Strong Ale	14	at 32.8	=	460

There remains of

	Barrels.	lb. gravity.		
2d Wort	12	at 20	=	240
3d Wort	14	at 6	=	84
Being	26	at 12.4	=	324

which is a good strength for small beer.

Other combinations might be made according to the sort of article that is required. Some brewers, for instance, might divide their worts in the following way:—

	Barrels.	lb. gravity.		
1st Wort	12	at 35	=	420
2d Wort	14	at 20	=	280
Strong Ale	26	at 26.9	=	700
and 3d Wort	14	at 6	=	84

for small beer. The strong ale, at nearly 27 lbs. gravity per barrel, is of the usual strength at which the London brewers make their sixty shillings ale, but those in the country will probably be surprised at the mention of 6 lbs. small beer. Persons who *wonder* know nothing of the metropolis. This strength would make very fair workhouse beer—fully as good as the price can afford. The excise duty is two shillings, and we have, nevertheless, known contracts for supplying some of those establishments, to which the beer was driven for miles and delivered at six shillings a barrel!

§ 3.—*Of making up Lengths.*

The necessity of boiling a wort longer than is otherwise requisite, for the purpose of raising its gravity, should be always guarded against, and seldom happens with experienced brewers. These can regulate their mashes so as to ensure the intended quantity and strength; but cases will occur, from various unforeseen circumstances, such as a mistake in the quality of the malt, where they must have recourse to a more than ordinary evaporation. In such cases, the saccharometer is the only guide. As an example, we shall suppose a brewing of porter, which, in London, is always made of an entire gyle, and, as nearly as possible, of the same strength. Let there be ten quarters of malt, from which the brewer expects 80 lbs. per quarter:—Of the black (or patent) malt, we take no account. The gravity of our porter must not be under 21 lbs., if we would keep up the character of the house. We have already cast the first and second worts, and the third is in the copper. A mash stands on the goods for a *Return*, but this can be of no service in the case before us:—We have, in the coolers,

	Barrels.	lbs.		Gravity.
1st Wort	12.5	at 32.5	=	406.2
2d Wort	13	at 20	=	260
Making	25.5	in weight	=	666.2

The third mash in the copper (allowing for the heat according to the Tables of Expansion which accompany the saccharometer) would, if cast now, amount to 16 barrels at 5 lbs. per barrel, being 80 lbs., the whole value of what remains in the copper. Adding this to the 666 lbs. already in the coolers, we find that the whole of the extract from the goods amounts only to 746 lbs. in place of the 800 lbs. which was expected. These 746 lbs. must be divided into barrels of 21 lbs. each; and, therefore, dividing by 21, we find that the quotient (35.5) is the whole quantity (*length* the brewers call it) which can be produced from this *gyle*. On looking back, we find that there are already 25½ of those barrels in the coolers; so that what worts are in the copper must be boiled down until, when cold, they shall not measure more than ten. There are 80 lbs. weight in the copper, and when boiled to 10 barrels, the gravity will be 8 lbs., for the evaporation is wholly aqueous. Suppose the operation finished, and we shall have—

	Barrels.	lbs.		gravity.
1st Wort	12.5	at 32.5	=	406.2
2d Wort	13	at 20	=	260
3d Wort	10	at 8	=	80
	35.5	at 21	=	746.2

In the preceding statement, we have mentioned a *Return*, without explaining the term. It was because we shall afterwards have to give directions on the subject. In the meantime we may state, generally, that it is a washing of the *goods*, which forms no part of the brewing of that day; but is preserved, with what strength it possesses, to be used as mashing liquor for the succeeding brewing.

CHAPTER VI.

Of the Materials of Ale and Beer.

At the present time, *ale* and *beer*, according to the will of the brewer, approach or recede from one another in their composition and consequent qualities, and are definable only in their extremes. We have reason to believe that our ancestors made a complete distinction: that, with them, *ale* was the pure wine of the malt, and that *beer* was *that* wine mixed with hops, or other bitter ingredients. In the improved edition of the " *Maison Rustique*," which was published in 1616, under the care of the industrious Gervase Markham, there are some useful remarks under the head of " *Brew-house*." Among many other things, he says that " the generall vse is by no means to put any *hops* into *ale* : making that the difference betwixt it and *beere*, that the one hath *hops*, the other none: but the wiser huswiues do find an error in that opinion, and say the vtter want of hops is the reason why ale lasteth so little a time, but either dyeth or soureth, and therefore they will to euery barrell of the best ale allow halfe a pound of good hops."

According to the present law, ale or beer, made for sale, must be composed entirely of malt and hops. Water is no doubt understood; but the qualities of the various kinds of those ingredients are left undetermined. We shall say something of each.

§ 1.—*Of Water.*

Pure water, although not a simple substance, is invariably the same; but it must be observed that the brewer never works with water that is pure: it is very unlikely that it would answer his purpose. If the saccharometer be made so as to sink to a certain point marked *zero* (a cypher) in distilled water, it will be found that every other liquor which

C 2

he can employ will show an infusion of something that marks, on his scale, a certain weight per barrel. What that something is he may not know; but as it appears in certain springs to the extent of a pound per barrel, it may, for aught he knows, have a material effect upon the result of his process. Further, the prohibitions of the Legislature are hereby often put at defiance, or thrown into ridicule; for, while the Excise-officer shall be threatening, or prosecuting, one brewer for putting a quarter of an ounce of sulphate of iron (copperas) into a barrel of his porter, another brewer, under the survey of the same officer, shall have ten times that quantity dissolved, naturally, in the water which supplies his brew-house. It is the same with carbonate of lime, common salt, and many other articles, which are strictly prohibited.

The carbonates of lime, magnesia, and potash, are powerful correctors of acidity, that plague of the brewery; but these are more frequent in *well* than in *river* water. The latter, especially that which comes from marshy grounds, is seldom to be chosen. The month of October, so famous from time immemorial for the manufacture of English beer, is that in which river water is most generally unfitted for use. It is then loaded with vegetable decompositions, and living animalculæ, neither of which are favourable to the vinous fermentation. The choice of water, therefore, if he be fortunate enough to have a choice, is a matter for serious consideration. Any solution that would affect the flavour of the ale will show itself in the taste of the water, which is then to be avoided without troubling ourselves with the analysis; but if there be nothing disagreeable either in taste, colour, or smell, and yet, notwithstanding, its specific gravity be markedly superior to that of distilled water, it is well to know what substance, or substances, it contains.

There have been, in all times, a contrariety of opinions among brewers concerning the adoption of *hard* or of *soft* water. *Hard water* is a term derived from culinary operations. It is such water as does not dissolve soap, and which is also ill-fitted for the extraction of the virtues of tea. *Soft water*, on the contrary, has both these qualities. Hard water is chiefly drawn from pit-wells. That which is the hardest contains sulphate of lime, which, by a double decomposition, separates the materials of the soap. With regard to its extractive power, this will probably depend upon the nature of the extract. In its application to malt, we have not discovered any deficiency in the quantity of produce. With regard to its effects on the beer, the sulphate of lime is not suspected to be in the slightest degree deleterious, and otherwise it is believed to be a preservative.

Another species of hard water is caused by the admixture of carbonate of lime, which is held in solution by means of an extra portion of carbonic acid. This is, however, less hard than the former; for it becomes *soft* by long boiling: the overplus carbonic acid is dissipated by the heat, and the pure carbonate of lime, being no longer soluble, is precipitated. It forms the incrustations that are so frequently seen on the insides of tea-kettles and other boilers. Whether this lime should be so precipitated before the liquor is used for mashing, has been much doubted by those brewers who have thought at all upon the subject. Lime is a favourite in the brewhouse. It is openly used, mixed with water, to preserve their wooden vessels from acidity, while they are unemployed in the summer months; and it is often put, by stealth, in the form of *marble dust*, *crabs' claws*, *egg shells*, &c., into their spring-brewed ales, for the purpose of absorbing the first germs of the acid fermentation.

§ 2.— *Of Malt.*

The juice of the grape, the sugar-cane, and many other vegetable substances, contain a great proportion of a sweet, or saccharine matter, ready formed; but the farinæ (or meal) of the common grains require to undergo some sort of operation before they become sweet. The process by which the grain acquires this taste, and which fits it for the use of the brewer, is termed *malting*. The barley, or other grain, becomes *malt*; that is, it is *mellowed*, or *sweetened*, so as to taste something like what the Latins called *mel*, and we term *honey*.

The ordinary process of malting is that of vegetation. The grain is first steeped in water until it has imbibed the moisture to its centre, and then spread on a floor, and turned from time to time, in quantities of various depths, according to the state of vegetation, which immediately commences. At a certain stage of the growth, the grain (which has been gradually becoming sweet) has acquired its maximum of *saccharification*. This, in barley, ordinarily occurs in two or three weeks, and is judged to take place at the moment when the *acrospire*, or rudiment of the future stalk, is ready to burst the shell. In other grain, the criterion is different; but we are not now writing a treatise upon *Malting*, although such a work is certainly wanted. The malt having arrived at this stage, is dried on a kiln, at a low, or a high heat, according as it is wanted to be pale, amber, or brown. Pale malt may be, and usually is, dried upon a hair-cloth, spread over wooden spars; but amber-coloured and brown malt require the floor of the kiln to be of iron-wire, or of perforated tiles. In either case, it is dried by means of the heated air passing through the malt and carrying the moisture along with it; and, therefore, when the empyreumatic flavour is guarded against, the fuel consists solely of coke, or other charcoal. In the case of amber, or brown malt, this care is not wanted, and hence the fire is made partially, if not wholly, of wood. The pyroligneous acid would thus pass through the malt; and there was once a time when the flavour so conveyed was supposed to be necessary to porter, for which those sorts of malt were solely manufactured. At the present time, porter for ordinary consumption is made wholly from pale malt; and a certain portion of *Patent Malt* (which is malt roasted like coffee, until it is *black*) is added for no other purpose but to produce the requisite colour.

This *conversion* of the mealy part of the grain into a sweet substance, or *saccharum*, and which has been called by some chemists the *Saccharine fermentation*, may be produced in a much more rapid manner than by the ordinary process of malting. If the grain be reduced to meal, in the manner stated under the section "*Grinding Machines*," and infused in water in the mash-tun (mixed up with a relatively small portion of ground malt); and if this infusion be kept for two or three hours, according to circumstances, at a heat of 150°, or nearly so, the whole mash will become saccharine: the fecula of the grain being as completely malted as if it had lain a fortnight on the malting floor. The proportion of malt is introduced as a *nidus* to hasten this fer-

mentation, on a similar principle as we put yeast into the worts which we would ferment into beer; or a portion of the *mother water* when we would turn the beer, or ale, into vinegar. The particulars of this manipulation will be given when we speak of the process of saccharification, or of brewing from unmalted grain.

§ 3.—*Of Hops.*

The general opinion of brewers, as well as of the public, is, that hops were first used in beer for the purpose of preserving it from acidity. This we doubt. Bitter ingredients, of various kinds, were used by our forefathers, before hops were considered proper for the purpose; and even the time is not very distant when these were supposed to be poisonous, and on that account prohibited by the legislator. We believe that, long ago, ale was made from malt alone; and that, when there was any fear for its preservation, a little honey was mixed with it, as is done at present in the South of France. The Herbalists, who were the *leeches* of those times, recommended certain plants as proper to be infused in the malt liquor, which was then termed *herb ale:* a denomination still known in various parts of the island. These herbs, like the medicaments of our own days, were generally the bitterest and most nauseous that could be found; but they cured diseases, and were, therefore, not only tolerated, but sought after; and, in process of time, some of them became necessary to certain tastes, and exist in the beer, or porter, which we now drink. Wine itself, when prescribed by the physician, is often medicated, serving as a vehicle for the introduction of the extracts of wormwood, quassia, gentian, and other bitter plants which, before their prohibition, were common in the brewhouse.

The culture of the hop is too well known to need any particular description in this place. There is only one species (*humulus lupulus*); but it has many varieties, which are chosen by the cultivators according as they are supposed to be most suited to the climate and soil. The plant is diœcious, and it is the female catkin which is picked and preserved for the brewer. Hops are strongly narcotic; but their bitter principle is the ostensible reason for their infusion in malt liquors.

The finer-flavoured and light-coloured

hops are pressed into sacks of comparatively fine cloth, called pockets, which weigh about a hundred weight and a half each, and are sold chiefly to the ale-brewer. The strong-flavoured and high-coloured hops are put into bags of a very coarse *mat-kind* of texture, called bags, and contain, generally, double the weight of the pockets. These are used by porter and small-beer brewers.

The bitter principle of hops is probably the same in all its varieties and modes of cultivation; but, in conjunction with this bitter, there is always, in new hops, a communicable flavour, or rather *aroma*, by which their several qualities are distinguished. Ale-brewers talk much of this aroma, and speak of its being concentrated in the essential oil of the hop, without considering that it must be, in a great degree, evaporated during the boiling of the worts. This aroma, like all others, is extremely evanescent. One of the best modes of preserving hops is to bury them among the dry malt; but, do what we will, the fine flavour does not exist a twelvemonth. Beyond that time they become *old hops;* and are sold at a cheaper rate to the porter-brewer. A year or two longer, and the *bitter itself* disappears; and the whole becomes nothing better than chaff. The same deterioration takes place when infused in the beer. The flavour is but of momentary duration; and the *bitter principle* gradually decays. In favour of those who believe that this bitter prevents acidity, it has been stated that the bitter is lost in proportion as the acidity is advanced. The loss of the one and the accession of the other are both, generally, the consequence of age; and it is well known that nothing is more easy than to mistake a concomitant circumstance for a cause. Thirty years ago, when we were young in the observance of the brewery, we formed a theory,—that the *bitter principle* was a substance *sui generis*, which, (while it lasted) by some chemical affinity, absorbed the acetous acid, gradually as it was formed. Subsequent experience has given us reason to suspect that this hypothesis is a dream.

It is the ale-brewer only who seeks for peculiarity of flavour in his hops. It is he who discriminates with nicety on the produce of the several counties; but his judgment varies with the taste of his customer. With respect to taste there is no criterion. It depends almost wholly on habit, otherwise we should find very few that could have a pleasure in chewing tobacco. The flavours of the different sorts of ale, however they are produced, are almost as various as the species of continental wines. The Burton, Wiltshire, Scotch, and London ales have little resemblance to one another, but each has its admirers. To be sure those varieties do not altogether depend upon the quality or quantity of the hops; but the infusion of this plant has always its share in the composition.

We believe that we cannot better conclude this section than by an extract from Mr. Richardson's work, formerly mentioned, which, though written thirty years ago, is not inapplicable to this present time:—

"The difference of soil has certainly a considerable influence in producing the real difference in flavour observable in hops. Those which grow on the stiff clays of Nottinghamshire, and are thence termed *North-clay hops*, have the pre-eminence in *rankness*, and accordingly, with a certain description of buyers, bear a higher price than Kent, though that is not so high as the general price of Farnham hops. To those who are not accustomed to the flavour of North-clay hops, they are undoubtedly rank, bordering on the nauseous, particularly whilst the beer brewed from them is new; and, indeed, that rankness generally remains a very considerable time, if not concealed by an abundant extract of malt. Hence they appear better adapted to strong-keeping beers, than to any other kind of malt-liquor.

"Farnham hops, however deserving the reputation they bear, are by no means worth the difference in price generally given for them, to a brewer, except the vicinity of his residence may, in some measure, lessen that difference; and it is not the intention of these pages to *appreciate* their value to the private consumer, with whom, perhaps, the idea of their incalculable excellence may have originated.

"The county of Kent, though justly claiming pre-eminent distinction in the produce of its hops, considered as uniting flavour with strength, is far from being uniform in its general priority, in this respect; for different parts produce different qualities, varying with the soil, or some other local circumstance, and all yielding the palm of superiority to those which grow in the neighbourhood of Canterbury.

"If, however, the rank austerity of the North-clay hops excites a nausea on the palate accustomed to the milder flavour of the Kentish, these, again, are as little relished by people who are in the habit of drinking ale in which Worcester hops only have been used. The flavour of these has a grateful mildness in it, not to be met with in any other hops. Hence the finest growths of Kent, in Lancashire, Cheshire, and some other counties, where the use of Worcester hops prevails, would be rejected as unsaleable; and so great is the objection of some of the inhabitants of those counties to the flavour of Kent hops, that I have heard them distinguish ale bittered with the latter, by the name of *Porter-ale*. Indeed, the distinction has propriety in it, so far as the strength of a large portion of these may convey to some palates the idea of *porter*, and that the mildness of the former can hardly be applicable to any liquor but *ale*."

§ 4.—*Of Isinglass.*

Although isinglass is not properly one of the materials of beer, being deposited as soon as it has performed its office of *fining*, yet, from its frequent employment and being the only ingredient that can be *legally* introduced into malt-liquor, we deem it not out of place in the present chapter.

"Fish-glue, as it is improperly called, is generally known by the name of *Isinglass*, a word corrupted from the Dutch *Hyzenblas*, an air-bladder, compounded of *hyzen*, to hoist, and *blas*, a bladder."

"It is chiefly prepared in the vicinity of the Caspian and Black Seas, from the *sounds*, or *swims*, of different species of the *acipenser*, or sturgeon. These bladders, stript of their outer rind and dried, constitute the isinglass of commerce. The skins, tails, &c., of these and other fishes are used for the inferior sorts of isinglass, but in no case are the materials boiled; for that would invariably convert them into glue, an article that has different qualities from those for which isinglass is required. Much of the latter, for instance, is used in making *Finings*, for the clarification of malt-liquors; whereas glue, added to turbid beer, would increase both its muddiness and its tenacity."[*]

In the brewery, isinglass is used solely as *finings*, that is, to clarify beer that is foul and muddy. In ale it is seldom necessary; but in porter, as commonly brewed, it cannot be dispensed with. Those sorts which are termed *long* and *short staple* (made from the larger and smaller fish respectively) being composed of single membranes that run parallel to each other, and are separable by infusion in cold water, are less liable to putrefaction; but the *Book-isinglass*, so called because it is folded somewhat in the shape of a book, is often found to be spoilt in its folds, from imperfect drying, which allows the generating of maggots, and consequent putrefaction. These spoilt parts should be carefully thrown aside.

The manufacture of isinglass was long exclusively confined to certain Russian provinces. In 1763 a patent was granted to a Mr. Jackson, for the preparation of "British isinglass," which was to be made from what he called "British materials"—but in reality from the entrails of sturgeons and other fish, imported from the American colonies, or caught on our own coasts. This undertaking was unsuccessful; for, in a well-written "Essay on British Isinglass," which Mr. Jackson published in 1765, he complains, that of 25 tons annually consumed in the brewery, he had only supplied a fourth, on account of certain prejudices that were raised against his article. These prejudices, however, no longer exist; for many of the large breweries now make use of nothing but the dried skins of soles.

Whatever sort of isinglass he employs, the brewer prepares his *finings* in the same manner:

It may be observed, that a pound of good isinglass will make about 12 gallons of the preparation. It may be used whole, but, for the sake of expedition, it is often bruised and pulled in pieces; then being put into a tub, with as much common vinegar as will cover it (or the same quantity of beer of any kind, which has acquired a considerable degree of acidity) the isinglass will swell and dissolve. As the whole thickens, there should be more beer added to it, and that of inferior acidity, because when the stronger acid has dissolved the isin-

---

[*] Booth's Analytical Dictionary of the English Language.

glass, almost any beer will serve to dilute and prepare it. This solution should be frequently stirred about briskly with an old stump broom, which separates the undissolved parts and makes it all of one consistence, which, finally, should be that of thin treacle. This is to be whisked through a hair sieve, or squeezed through a coarse linen cloth, into another tub, previous to using it. The quantity to be used is from a pint to a quart per barrel, according to the degree of feculency in the beer. This should be made quite thin with some of the beer intended to be purified, whisking it up till it froths. It is then to be poured into the cask, and stirred briskly about in it, bunging it down immediately, and the beer will become pure in about 24 hours, provided it has been in a condition proper to receive the finings.

An eligible mode of discovering whether beer be in a proper state to yield to finings or not is the following :—

"Draw off a little of the beer into a pint, or half-pint phial, and add to it about half a tea-spoonful of the finings. Shake it up, and then let it remain stationary. If the finings will have the desired effect, you will observe, in a few minutes, the isinglass collecting the feculencies of the beer into large fleecy masses, which will begin regularly to subside to the bottom. If the beer be not in a proper state, (which is ever the case as long as the fermentation continues, or an after *fret* prevails,) the bulk of the finings will soon be at the bottom, leaving the beer neither pure nor foul, except just at the top, where there will be a little transparency, perhaps a quarter of an inch deep, which will grow deeper in time, but will not readily extend to the whole."

The mode in which isinglass acts upon the feculencies of beer has been variously estimated. The general idea is, that it spreads over the surface of the liquor, and then falling by its weight, carries down the foul parts, allowing the pure beer to ascend, as if strained through a sieve. On the contrary, it seems to us that its effect is owing to that indescribable cause termed chemical attraction. The observations of Mr. Jackson, formerly mentioned, lead directly to this result. According to him, isinglass is never *perfectly* dissolved in the acid liquor, otherwise it would cease to act as *finings*. These, however intimately mixed with any dissolvent, must always preserve a fibrous form; for says he, "Any substance which appears horny, breaks short, or snaps like glue, although it dissolves like isinglass, and puts on the appearance of a rich thick jelly, the universal characteristic of good fining, yet will not fine down beer." The isinglass and the acid beer are then only mechanically, not chemically united. If the latter, they would become a species of glue; and such, finings will become, if exposed even to a very moderate degree of heat, perhaps at 90° or 100°. They should, therefore, be kept cool. "That common finings," says the same author, "is nothing more than a due division, or an imperfect solution of isinglass in subacid liquors, may be proved, by viewing it through magnifying glasses, or by admixing a few drops of fining with fair water in a glass, which being held up to the light, the fibres may be seen swimming in an infinite variety of forms and sizes, and, on subsiding, arrange themselves according to their different gravities, the smallest particles of which, perceptible to the eye, attract each other, and form an appearance of little clouds. If then we take this mixture, and warm it at the fire, we shall presently find, that all these fibres will escape perception, in being perfectly dissolved, except a few gross parts. The same phenomena appear, if we place a little fining near the fire, or hold a lump a few minutes in the palm of the hand; *thus the constituence will be broken, the fibres dissolved, and the efficacy destroyed.*"

The *rationale* of the action of finings, according to the author just quoted, is this :—"It is evident that at the very instant that fining is commixed with beer to be clarified, the stale beer, in which the isinglass was dissolved, or divided, quits the fibres and unites with the body of the beer; while at the same time the fibres, now set loose, and everywhere interspersed in the beer, attract and unite with the loose feculent particles, which, before this union, being of the same specific gravity with the beer, could not possibly subside alone, but by this reciprocal attraction having obtained an additional weight, are now rendered proportionably heavier, and precipitate together of course, in form of the curdly magma just mentioned. But it sometimes happens, from certain inadvertencies in brewing, and mismanagement in the cellar afterwards, that beer turns out specifically heavier than the fibres of the isinglass; in which case the fining cannot subside, for the reasons aforesaid, but floats at the surface: at other times, notwithstanding the union of the fibres and feculencies, the combined matter becoming exactly of the same weight as the beer, continues interspersed everywhere in it, and neither emerges nor subsides; in both instances the beer is nicknamed *stubborn* by the coopers."

Chapter VII.

Of Illegal Ingredients.

ALTHOUGH water, malt, hops, and isinglass are the only materials which can be legally employed in the manufacture of malt-liquors brewed for sale, yet, as the prohibitory clause is but of modern date, and many other articles have been wont, from time immemorial, to be added to beer, which are not only innoxious, but occasionally advantageous, and are still left to the discretion of the private brewer, we have judged it proper to class them together in the present chapter. In doing so, we shall distribute those which have been most commonly used into five divisions:—

1. Such ingredients as are intended to increase the quantity of saccharine matter, or strength of the worts; and, consequently, to save malt.
2. Such ingredients as are intended to increase the quantity of the bitter principle; and, consequently, to save hops.
3. Such ingredients as are intended to prevent the introduction of acidity; or to diminish or destroy that acidity when it is already formed.
4. Such ingredients as are intended to add an extraneous flavour to ale, or beer, so as to accommodate it to the taste of the inhabitants of any particular district, who have been accustomed to that flavour. And,
5. Such ingredients as are intended solely for the purpose of increasing the intoxicating quality of ale, or beer, and which are, in almost all cases, of too poisonous a nature to be introduced with safety.

On the principal articles in each of these divisions we shall make a few remarks, and then leave their introduc-

tion, or rejection, to the judgment of the brewer: premising, in the outset, that various and very different flavours may be given, in the process of fermentation, to ale which is manufactured from malt and hops alone.

§ 1.—*Of Ingredients which are intended to increase the quantity of Saccharine Matter, or Strength of the Worts.*

Of all the substitutes for malt, raw grain is the principal—if, indeed, that can be called a substitute which is merely malted in the mash-tun in place of the floor. The process by which the conversion of barley, or other grain, into malt is thus rapidly performed will be detailed in a subsequent chapter. While we warn the public brewer of the *legal* danger of its adoption, we would strenuously recommend its use in private families. Were the practice to become general, a deduction of the duties on beer made for sale would inevitably follow.

Pure sugar and water (it has been said) will not ferment; but raw sugar, or molasses, will make very good beer either alone, or mixed with malt-worts. There is, however, no saving from the use of these materials, unless when malt becomes much dearer than in ordinary years: in which case they are occasionally permitted to be used under the authority of the Lords of the Treasury. A weak beer from molasses is frequently made in private families, and drunk in a half-fermented state; but it is too luscious for the taste of those who are accustomed to the small beer of malt. Molasses, mixed with a weak malt-wort, would, when fermented, be much more palatable.

Our ancestors, as well as other northern nations, were much accustomed to a vinous liquor from honey, which vied with the wines of the south: the *methu* of the Greeks, the *medu* of the Saxons, the *hydromel* of the Latins, and the *mead*, or *metheglin*, of more modern times. The extension of agriculture, which by diminishing the food of bees raised the price of honey, conjoined with the excise-duty imposed, has completely annihilated the manufacture of mead for sale, and even in private families it is now seldom or never to be seen. Honey, however, is still used in the private brewing of ale; and in some districts it is clandestinely introduced by the public brewer. The design and effect of this introduction will be afterwards explained. It is almost unnecessary to add that honey is not deleterious.

Liquorice root, (*Glycyrrhiza glabra*,) both in powder and in the state of extract (*Spanish juice*), was formerly an essential constituent of malt-liquors, and particularly of porter. We believe, however, that the saving of malt was less considered in this article than its flavour. At all events the introduction in the copper of about half-a-pound per barrel, and that quantity was seldom exceeded, must have been perfectly harmless.

§ 2.—*Of Ingredients which are intended to increase the quantity of the bitter principle, and in consequence to save hops.*

That hops prevent ale from becoming acid is, if true, a comparatively modern discovery. Mum, (a malt-liquor now unknown in England,) although directed to be kept two years before it was tapped, contained no species of bitter among its numerous ingredients; and the beer of Louvain, so famous throughout France, is brewed without hops. It is well-known that bitter infusions themselves, without any other vegetable matter, will become sour.

The use of bitters followed the advice of the physician, who, being anciently a herbalist, recommended the plants that grew in his garden. Each plant had its particular disease which it was able to combat; and hence the whole science of medical botany. According to those gentlemen, the bitter principle was, and still is, peculiarly efficacious. "It is a pure *tonic*,—increases the appetite,—promotes digestion,—gives vigour to the system, &c." Unfortunately for this general eulogium, the bitters are either different in their essence, or they are never pure. A few, such as gentian and quassia, are, comparatively, inactive. Some, like aloes and marsh trefoil, are purgative. Hops are astringent and narcotic; broom and some others are diuretics: while many, as opium, cocculus indicus, ignatia amara, tobacco and nux vomica, are highly poisonous. Yet each of those here mentioned, and others which we have not named, have been boiled among the worts of beer, without regard to their effect on particular constitutions, or to the general safety of the individuals for whom the liquor is brewed.

These observations being premised, our account of the substitutes for hops may be short. Broom, wormwood, and several other bitters, are now almost universally laid aside; for, since the flavour of the hops has been so generally recognized, no bitter which is inconsistent with that flavour would be relished. Bitters that are perfectly, or at least nearly, flavourless may, indeed, be added to hops when the bitter principle only is required; and this is the case with porter, in which *flavour is little studied:* for the hops usually employed in brewing that beverage are either coarse, or old, and would not be admissible in fine ales. The cocculus indicus, so frequently introduced into the latter, has a taste by no means agreeable; but its intoxicating quality is all that is wanted by the brewer, and, could that be procured (as has been attempted) in an isolated state, its flavour would be willingly dispensed with.

The bitter contained in porter is very great, and if taken wholly from hops, must require an average quantity of ten or twelve pounds to the quarter of malt, or about three pounds per barrel. The fluctuation in the price of that article is extreme, as will appear from the following statement, which was printed in 1819, by order of the House of Commons. The quality here mentioned is *bag hops*, which are the cheapest in the market.

1789	Oct.	6*l.* 14*s.*	to	7*l.*	2*s.*	per cwt.
1790	Oct.	76*s.*	—	84*s.*		—
1791	Oct.	5*l.* 5*s.*	—	5*l.* 12*s.*		—
1792	Oct.	80*s.*	—	84*s.*		—
1793	Oct.	9*l.* 9*s.*	—	10*l.* 0*s.*		—
1794	Oct.	84*s.*	—			—
1795	Oct.	5*l.* 0*s.*	—	5*l.* 12*s.*		—
1796	Oct.	80*s.*	—	84*s.*		—
1797	Mar.	112*s.*	—	120*s.*		—
1797	Oct.	84*s.*	—	90*s.*		—
1798	Oct.	9*l.* 9*s.*	—	10*l.* 0*s.*		—
1799	Nov.	14*l.* 14*s.*				—
1801	Jan.	16*l.* 5*s.*	—	18*l.* 0*s.*		—
1802	Jan.	5*l.* 5*s.*				—
1803	July	5*l.* 12*s.*				—
1804	July	4*l.* 15*s.*	—	5*l.* 0*s.*		—
1812	Nov.	13*l.* 13*s.*	—	15*l.* 5*s.*		—
1813	Jan.	13*l.* 13*s.*	—	15*l.* 10*s.*		—
1814	Dec.	9*l.* 4*s.*	—	9*l.* 9*s.*		—
1815	Feb.	8*l.* 16*s.*	—	9*l.* 9*s.*		—
1816	July	6*l.* 10*s.*	—	6*l.* 17*l.*		—
1816	Oct.	14*l.* 14*s.*				
1817	Jan.	14*l.* 5*s.*				
1818	Jan.	31*l.* 0*s.*				

It is not to be wondered at, that, under these circumstances, substitutes should have been sought for with avidity. If the substitutes were not more noxious than the principal, (and some of them were less so,) the conscience of the brewer was easily satisfied: especially seeing that he could procure as much bitter for sixpence as would otherwise have cost him a pound.

Marsh trefoil, buckbean, or *bogbean* (*Menyanthes trifoliata*), has been employed in place of hops,—openly on the continent, and privately, (at one time,) as has been said, in this country. The leaves were collected, when mature, and dried in the shade, to preserve their colour. They were then well boiled and scummed to free them from their excess of roughness; and the remaining extract was preserved and put into the fermenting tun in such proportions as the brewer judged proper, or as his druggist chose to direct. These leaves have very nearly the flavour of the hop; and an ounce of the former is said to be equivalent to half-a-pound of the latter. It should be observed, however, for the guidance of any one who shall dare to use them, that although they stand recommended in the modern pharmacopœias, the quantity of a drachm taken in powder "purges and vomits."

Aloes (the dried juice of the ALOE *perfoliata*) is a well known bitter, being much used in medicine. When it was allowed to be sold to brewers, the variety *succotrina* was always preferred, as having the least objectionable smell. The quantity which could be mixed with the hops in the copper was limited, in consequence of its purgative quality, and seldom exceeded half an ounce to a barrel of porter.

Quassia is another well-known bitter; it is the favourite of the physician, and would be equally so of the porter-brewer, if he dared to use and acknowledge it. The smell, if any, is imperceptible, and the bitter is intense, pure, and lasting. The *quassia amara* (a shrub) is the most biting of the tribe; but that commonly imported into this country, from the West Indies, is the bark and wood of the root and trunk of the *quassia excelsa*, which is a large tree. When the porter-brewers made use of quassia, it was either in small chips or rasped, and put into the copper (with the hops) in a quantity of about an ounce to the barrel. This is, probably, the most harmless of all the illegal bitters. The physicians prescribe the decoction to their patients to the extent of a quarter of an ounce of the bark a day,—as much as the brewer was accustomed to put into nine gallons of his porter.

There are other bitter ingredients worth noticing; but as they are intended for purposes different from the saving of hops, they belong more properly to the succeeding divisions of this chapter.

§ 3.—*Of Ingredients which are intended to prevent the introduction of acidity, or to diminish or destroy that acidity when it is already formed.*

It would not be difficult to account for the action of the greater number of the ingredients of this description, upon the principles of modern chemistry. Nevertheless, it is certain that all those articles were in use, for the same purpose, centuries before the present theories of acetification had existence. Practice always precedes theory. The latter merely strings together the facts that have been previously (often accidentally) discovered. It was known, from time immemorial, that ale, or beer, when exposed to the atmosphere, especially in summer, became rapidly sour; and hence the closeness of the casks, and the coolness of the cellars, were as much attended to in former as in latter times. It was also known that certain salts, (as they were called,) and certain earths, were preventives if not remedies: in short, we know little or nothing that is new upon the subject.

Common salt, so useful in preventing the putrefaction of animal substances, was also believed to have a similar effect in the preservation of vegetables; and, accordingly, we find the condemnation of its use among the earliest restrictive laws of the brewery. Different opinions exist with respect to its utility; but, however these may be decided, it can scarcely be suspected to be dangerous. Publicans have been accused of putting it in the beer to produce thirst; and we have known private gentlemen, who prided themselves on the quality of their *home-brewed*, throw in about a pound per barrel into the casks with the view of flavour. Many brewers mix salt with wheat or bean flour, putting a handful in each cask before cleansing, to promote the discharge of the yeast; and, occasionally, the same mixture of flour and salt, or flour and *saltpetre*, or *salt prunella*, is introduced into the tun to rouse a languid fermentation.

That the fermentation should not linger between a nauseous sweet and a vinous flavour, is reckoned essential to the prevention of acidity. The extent to which it should be carried will be considered hereafter, but we now speak of such ingredients as are supposed to excite the working when it is too languid. *Jalap*, to the extent of two, or even three ounces, to twenty barrels, is employed by certain brewers in the gyle-tun, but the *rationale* of its action is to us unknown.

The formation of vinegar, like other fermentations, proceeds more rapidly when it has a *nidus* or incipient acidity from which to begin. In the aërial theory, that *nidus* is oxygen; and to destroy or counteract this oxygen in the outset is to strangle the demon in the moment of its birth.

When the fermentation is finished in a proper manner, it remains with the brewer to keep the casks, if possible, hermetically sealed, to prevent the admission of the external air. Bottles are still better than casks. When laid on their sides, so as to keep the corks swelled, nothing can enter from without; and the sole danger is, when the liquor retains so much of undecomposed saccharine matter as to cause the bursting of the vessel from a new fermentation. It is on this account that beer, when it is to be bottled, is usually exposed for a time to the atmosphere, by loosening the bung, in order to *flatten* it; that is, to facilitate the escape of the carbonic acid which it then contains. During this exposure, while the fixed air escapes, a portion of the atmospheric air may enter; and with the view of preventing this, it is the practice of some, who affect the mysteries of the trade, to pour about two ounces of the *spirit of Maranta* into the cask, which is then allowed to stand, without the bung, for three or four days before bottling. How this can exclude one gas and allow another to escape, we know not, having never personally made the experiment. This fiery liquid is a spirituous extract of the medicinal root *Galangal:*—the *Kœmpferia galanga, Alpinia galanga, Amomum galanga,* and *Maranta galanga,* of different botanists.

The exclusion of the atmospheric air, by covering the surface of the liquid, has been managed in different ways. The small wine, when carried out to the Italian vintagers, is in weak flasks, which would not bear the pressure of a cork. These have long necks, and the surface of the liquor is covered with a film of olive oil, which swims on the fluid, and is easily separated afterwards by means of a little cotton. The handful of half-boiled hops, impregnated with wort, which is usually put into the bunghole of each cask by the ale-brewer when stowing it in his cellar, answers the same purpose : and some, more rigidly attentive, insert (privately) at the same time, about an ounce of powdered black rosin, previously mixed with beer, which swims on the surface, but after a time is partially absorbed. Of this we shall have again to speak when we treat of *Burton ale*.

Bruised *green Copperas*, called also *salt of steel,* (*sulphate of iron*) which has always been put into porter—formerly by the brewer and now by the publican—is, ostensibly, for the purpose of giving it a *frothy top*. It is either used alone, or mixed with *alum,* and is technically called *heading*. The quantity used need not exceed as much as would lie on a half-crown piece for a barrel, and to that extent there is no danger to be feared. This practice, we believe, had been originally intended to keep the beer alive during the time in which it remained in the pots. The *green* sulphate of iron is greedy of oxygen, and is thereby speedily converted into the *brown*. We apprehend that it is in consequence of this dissolved salt of iron, that certain porter-drinkers have uniformly asserted that there is a peculiar flavour when drinking out of a tin pot, which does not exist when taken from a glass : if this be true, the effect will naturally be referred to galvanic influence.

The brewers, in one quarter of the island, are in the practice of putting sulphate of iron (previously dried to whiteness) in the liquor of their first mash. This is probably meant to guard against that species of acetification termed *blinking ;* but its effect must be little, since the quantity is limited to about two ounces for twenty barrels of liquor.

Some ingredients are introduced which lie dormant or deposited in the cask, for the purpose of catching and neutralizing the acetous acid at the moment of its formation. The chief of these is *lime* under various forms. Quick lime does not answer this end. It is partly soluble, and, in so far, communicates a disagreeable taste. The carbonates, if pure, are free from this fault; and therefore, *marble dust* and powdered *oyster shells* have been generally used. Before any vinegar exists in the beer, these carbonates of lime usually lie at the bottom of the cask inactive; but on the least degree of acetification an acetate of lime is formed and the carbonic acid escapes. The acetate of lime is soluble, and, in proportion as it is formed, the flavour of the beer is altered. It remains, therefore, with the drinker, whether he prefers this new bitterish taste to that of the acetous acid which would otherwise predominate.

We have here supposed that the carbonate of lime will remain inactive until acetous acid shall be formed; but it may possibly be otherwise. An excess of carbonic acid would render it soluble, but the same effect would follow with respect to its union with the vinegar. This soluble super-carbonate of lime, if effected, would not be discernible by the palate; for it often exists plentifully in water without being thus observed. Besides, this extra absorption of carbonic acid would tend to prevent the secondary fermentation, which is the usual precursor of acidity.

Egg-shells and even whole eggs are sometimes introduced into beer, in which they act the same part as the carbonates of lime. The shells are, in fact, almost wholly the same substance. The following *recipe*, which was first published in an early number (the 27th) of the Philosophical Transactions, shows that the use of eggs for the prevention of acidity is of no modern date. The writer (Dr. Stubbs) says that *he learned it from an ale-seller in Deal*, and that he tried it, successfully, in a voyage to Jamaica. "To every runlet of five gallons, after it is placed in the ship not to be stirred any more, put in two new-laid eggs whole, and let them lie in it; in a fortnight, or little more, the whole egg-shells will be dissolved, and the eggs become like wind-eggs, inclosed only in a thin skin; after this the white is preyed on, but the yolks are not touched or corrupted, by which means the ale was so well preserved, that it was found better at Jamaica than at Deal." It may be observed, that although this was new to Dr. Stubbs, he was not the original discoverer. It was probably known *in the trade* for centuries.

Sulphate of lime, which is partly soluble in water, is put into the cask, after it has ceased working, for the purpose of preventing an *after-fret*. If it effect this end, it is well; but at any rate, the quantity of six ounces to a barrel cannot possibly do harm.

Hartshorn shavings, to the extent of six pounds for twenty barrels, were *formerly* boiled in the worts of the best London ale. These give out *ammonia* by distillation, and consist chiefly of *phosphate of lime*, with a considerable quantity of gelatine. These shavings are probably expected to prevent acidity, but we are at a loss to know how. The ammonia is evaporated, and the phosphate, even were it to act like the carbonate, can scarcely be extracted by boiling.

According to Pliny, the Gauls were able to preserve their beer for many years. We fear that they have lost the secret; but we shall just notice some of the means to which they still have recourse, and which are not practised in this country.

The common Avens, or *Herb Bennet*, (*Geum Urbanum*,) is highly extolled all over the continent, for its medicinal, as well as other valuable properties. It was hence, perhaps, that it acquired the surname of *bennet*, or *benet*, contracted from *benedictus*, although the origin is now ascribed to a Saint of that name. The roots of this plant, particularly when it grows on a dry, sandy soil, have a pleasant odour, (similar to that of cloves,) which it readily imparts to any spirituous menstruum. On this account it is highly valued by the brewers; and is said to be a prominent ingredient in the *Augsburg Beer*, which is so famous throughout Germany. The dried roots are sliced, and inclosed in a thin linen bag, which is suspended in the store-vat, or cask; and it is asserted, with what truth we know not, that the beer so managed never becomes acid.

In former times (and the custom is not yet completely laid aside) the real, or imaginary preventives of acidity were inserted into the cask, along with the *Finings*; or rather, the whole mixture passed generally under the latter denomination. It will be shown, when we speak of the process of *Saccharification*, that the portion of unfermented worts, which always remains in the beer, is often more allied to starch than to sugar; and, in that case, it is frequently the cause,—not only of *foulness*, but of subsequent acidity. On examining the accounts of old processes for the brewing and cellaring of beer, it is curious to observe their consonance with the chemical announcements of later times. We now know that malt-extract is a mixture of *Starch* and *Saccharum*, and that the former is capable of being deposited by an infusion of *Nutgalls*. The following directions for the manufacture of beer-finings were published in a highly respectable French work, nearly a century ago; and then given as an *old* and general practice among the brewers in Paris:—

Take three pounds of powdered nut-galls and four ounces of potash. Boil these for three hours in such a quantity of water as, at the end of that time, will make the weight of the whole mixture about twelve pounds. To this, when cool, add two pints of spirit of wine; and, after it has settled and become clear, bottle it up for use. Five ounces of this decoction will be sufficient to fine and preserve half a piece of beer.

When the ale or beer becomes really sour, we know not how to extract its oxygen. He who shall discover this will make his fortune. If even the vinegar itself could be deposited, the strength of the remaining beer might be restored; but though the acidity can be neutralized by means of the *sub-carbonates of potash* and *soda*, which, with other similar articles, are hawked about as *nostrums* among the publicans, the acetous salts still remain dissolved, and contaminate the mass. Attempts are sometimes made to cover the disagreeable taste, by the introduction of *sugar-candy*,—a substance not readily fermentable,—but, even setting aside the trouble and expense, the beer *thus said to be recovered* (although not pernicious) is never pleasing to the drinker.

§ 4.—*Of Ingredients which are intended to add an extraneous Flavour to the Ale or Beer.*

The most agreeable, and, at the same time, the most permanent flavours of malt liquors are those which are formed by the particular modes of fermentation. In addition to these, however, certain extraneous ingredients have been introduced, by individual brewers, which have given a character to their ales; and even whole districts have adopted peculiarities of taste which would by no means pass generally in other quarters. When those ingredients are confined to this single object, their introduction, though legally wrong, is not morally vicious; and we shall, therefore, mention a few which have been most usually employed.

The dried root of the *sweet flag* (*Acorus calamus*), commonly termed *Calamus aromaticus*, is warm, slightly bitter, and has been extolled beyond all other British plants for its aromatic flavour. This root is usually imported from the Levant, but does not appear to be superior to the growth of our own country.

Coriander seeds (*Coriandrum sativum*) are imported for the use of the brewer, as well as for medicinal purposes. The plant is found wild in this country, but is a doubtful native.

Carraway (the seeds of the *Carum carui*) have also been used in brewing, but not so frequently as the *coriander*, which some believe to add strength as well as flavour. *Carraway* is also found wild in England, and, along with the *coriander*, it is cultivated, in some counties, for the use of confectioners and apothecaries.

The three ingredients last mentioned have, no doubt, been chosen on account of their warm aromatic flavours. All have been boiled together in the copper; the first *sliced*, in the proportion of four pounds to twenty barrels, and the two latter *ground*,—about two pounds each to the same quantity of ale.

Various other stimulating roots and seeds have been made use of: *Orange peel*, powdered, is very generally used by the ale-brewers of this country; as also Orange peas, or Curaçoa oranges, the unripe fruit of the *Citrus aurantium*. Vegetables of a spicy and more stimulating taste are likewise in general use. Of these, we may mention *Long pepper* (*Piper longum*); *Capsicum*, or *Guinea pepper* (*Capsicum annuum*); *Grains of paradise* (*Amomum granum*); common *Ginger* (*Amomum zingiber*), &c. One or all of these foreign seeds and roots are powdered and boiled among the worts, in quantities of about three pounds to twenty barrels: the quantity being regulated by the degree of pungency required.

§ 5.—*Of Ingredients which are intended solely for the purpose of increasing the intoxicating power of Beer or Ale.*

Hitherto we have treated of ingredients which, though illegal, (and, in our opinion, calculated only to gratify an acquired taste,) are at least harmless: but we have now to speak of articles that deserve no quarter,—of such as are disgraceful to the brewer, because dangerous to the drinker.

The dried fruit of the *Menispermum cocculus*, better known by the names of *India berry* and *Cocculus Indicus*, claims, on account of its very general use, the first place in this infernal list. Its importation into this country (from the East Indies) is very great, considering that few know for what other purpose it is ever used: for, though the *Cissampelos pareira* (which many botanists state to be the same plant) has a place in the pharmacopœias, its virtues are generally referred to the root, and that root is brought from America. That *Cocculus Indicus* is a strong narcotic is doubtless; for it is on that account alone that it has preserved its place in the brewery. In India the berries are thrown into the water for the purpose of catching fish, which, by swallowing them, become intoxicated. They were once used in England in the same way, but, we believe, that practice is now prohibited. Their effects upon the human frame we know not, neither do we wish to know.

The extensive use of this ingredient (and we have good reason to believe that it is still used extensively) was proved to a Committee of the House of Commons in 1818. Those who give brewing receipts recommend it in quantities of four pounds to twenty barrels, boiled with the worts: but there seems to be a mystery on this subject which requires to be investigated.

The *Faba amara*, or *bitter bean*, is the seed of an East India plant, which, though poisonous, has a sanctified name. It is the *Ignatia amara, St. Ignatius's bean*, and is not only botanically, but naturally allied to the genus *Strychnos*, a species of which will come next under our review. The *bitter bean* appears in many of the works that pretend to teach the art of Brewing. It is a large pear-shaped berry, with seeds nearly an inch long, and extremely bitter.

Nux vomica (*Strychnos nux vomica*), as described by the botanists, " is the fruit, or rather seed of the fruit, or berry, of a large tree, growing in Egypt, Ceylon, &c. of a strong narcotic quality, so as to be ranked in the number of poisons." " It is round and flat, about an inch broad and near a quarter of an inch thick," — " extremely bitter, but with little or no smell." " Ignatius's bean partakes of the same qualities."

We suspect that what was at one time generally sold to brewers for *Cocculus Indicus* was really *Nux vomica;* and that the numerous body of quacks who called themselves brewers' druggists, and who were *almost* annihilated by Exchequer prosecutions about ten or twelve years ago, passed the *Faba amara* and *Nux vomica* under the name of *Cocculus Indicus*, when making their defence, on the same principle as the forgers of bank-notes are accustomed to plead guilty to the lesser indictment. In the examination of Mr. Carr, the Solicitor of Excise, before the House of Commons, in the document formerly mentioned, we have the following words:

" Is it [*Cocculus Indicus*] a bulky commodity, or is it easy to be smuggled ?—It is of the size of a pretty large nut; every piece of it is about the size of a nut. It bears the poisonous principle so strongly in it, that by an analysis it is very easily separated from the substance, and is produced in the form of a crystal. Now, if any druggist would take the trouble to do that, it would be possible to take as small a quantity as a thimblefull, which would poison a great deal of beer."

Now this description agrees with the appearance of nux vomica, but by no means with that of cocculus Indicus, which is, originally, about the bulk of a black currant, but being dry when brought to this country, is of a much smaller size.

Opium is another ingredient which was formerly sold, under different disguises, by those gentlemen druggists, and which, we have reason to believe, is still in use; for we have known seizures of that article in the custody of ale-brewers, within the last two years. A compound termed *multum* was (or *is*) a mixture of opium and other ingredients, which sold about ten years ago, at five or six shillings a pound, when what was called an *extract of cocculus* was charged at a guinea and a-half. *Tobacco*, too, has been made use of, but how disguised we have not learned.

It will be said that every article which we have here stigmatized is medicinal, and appears in the pharmacopœias; but we also know that there is no substance, however deleterious or disgusting, which has not, at one time or other, found a place in the *Materia medica*. Besides, the parallel is imperfect. In medicine the poison is prescribed in measured doses, (less or more, according to the prudence or the rashness of the physician,) and only in such diseases as are otherwise deemed incurable; whereas the brewer, or his drayman, administers the drugs without discrimination, ignorant and careless of the age, sex, or constitution of his patient.

In the tone of reprehension, which we have felt it our duty to assume on this subject, we trust that we shall not be accused of personality. Let it be remembered that we address ourselves to the most worthless of the trade, to such as disgrace the name of brewer, by sporting with the lives of their fellow-creatures, for the sake of gain.* If there be any honest man so weak as to suppose that we mean to throw suspicion upon the brewery in general, we wish him to be undeceived. We are willing to believe that the number of reckless beings who use deleterious ingredients are few; but that there exist those few, is too well ascertained, from the seizures and convictions that have been so often made, and are still making, by the Excise. Our denunciations are directed solely against the guilty; and sorry should we be, if they could possibly be conceived to allude to any respectable House, or to any honourable man.

* See Coroner's Inquest in the *Times Newspaper* of the 29th of June last.

THE ART OF BREWING.

PART II.

PRACTICAL INSTRUCTIONS

CHAPTER

Introductory.

THE *practical instructions* for brewing ale and beer, as given by different persons, are by no means uniform. The cause is obvious. The mode of manufacture, and consequently the quality, differ in every age and country; and, even in the same nation, the ale of one district has little resemblance to that of another. The London, Burton, Wiltshire, and Scotch ales are each remarkably distinguishable; and the instructions which are privately given to young brewers, take their tone from the quarter where the instructor has been bred. He who has seen only one of the modes of brewing, can have no conception of their number and variety. One shall mash three or four times, while another shall do so but once. A second shall pitch his tun at 80°, when others do so at 45°, the former cleansing in twenty-four hours, and the latter waiting three or four weeks for the finishing of the fermentation. One class of brewers attend chiefly to the attenuation, are minute in their heats of fermentation, weighing the yeast with the utmost care; while there are many gentlemen (at the same time, priding themselves on the goodness of their ale) who turn the worts into the barrels boiling hot, bung them up, and stow them for a year in their cellars, without any yeast at all. Each of these modes of brewing may be considered as producing a different species of ale; and each species has its varieties depending on natural or accidental circumstances, (such as the water, and the skill of the brewer,) which add to its preservative qualities, and give certain adventitious flavours. Porter is a peculiar species of malt liquor, and possesses a general uniformity of taste and strength: but this, too, differs in its kind; for, although confined in its manufacture almost exclusively to ten or twelve houses, an experienced palate is at no loss to distinguish that of any one house from all the others.

From what we have now stated, it is obvious that we can give no *general set of instructions* which shall apply to brewing as an abstract science. We shall, therefore, separate our directions into divisions, suitable to those species of malt liquors, with the brewing of which we are best acquainted, but without affecting, in any way, to exhaust the subject; for we have found, experimentally, during the course of twenty years, that there have occurred to us many things of which our philosophy had not dreamed.

The press has hitherto furnished very little information on the subject of brewing. Mr. Richardson's work, formerly mentioned, contains many useful *theoretical hints*; but it was not his intention to publish *practical rules*. These he reserved for private communication, by which he secured a much greater reward than usually falls to the lot of authors. His pupils were numerous; and his method of brewing, in consequence, forms one of the divisions with which the reader ought to be made acquainted. It varies extremely from that of the Scotch; and although he treats of Burton ale, his method, certainly, is not the mode by which ale could be made like the Burton of the present day. In our opinion, his directions for porter are unexceptionable, as far as they go; but that article is now very different from what it once was, and what it might be. At all events, Mr. Richardson's instructions, being very minute, will serve us for general reference, when we speak of other kinds of malt liquor; and, therefore, we shall copy them, without alteration, from a manuscript for which he was paid a hundred and fifty guineas, besides receiving a guarantee of secrecy for twenty years. Previously, however, it will be necessary to make a few remarks upon those changes which vegetables undergo, when they are understood to be submitted to what have been termed the *Saccharine* and the *Vinous fermentations*.

Chapter II.

Of the Saccharine Fermentation, *or the Extraction of Worts from Raw Grain, and other Vegetables.*

Whether or not the *saccharum*, or sweet, of vegetables be identically the same, wherever it is found, has not been, and perhaps cannot be, ascertained. That of the sugar-cane and the beet-root is equally crystallizable and undistinguishable; but there are many other saccharine extracts which it has hitherto been attempted in vain to crystallize. To the brewer, however, they have all one principle in common. Saccharine infusions, from whatever vegetables they may be drawn, are capable of undergoing a fermentation, during which carbonic acid is evolved; the liquid becomes of less specific gravity, acquires a vinous flavour, and gives out alcohol by distillation. These are the essential characteristics of a *sweet extract;* so much so that, instead of *saccharine*, it is more generally termed *fermentable, matter.* Indeed, this is the more appropriate denomination; for, should any vegetable *sweet* be found that is incapable of this chemical change, it would necessarily require to be arranged in a different division of vegetable substances.

The saccharine matter of plants is often found ready formed in their juices, during certain periods of their growth, or in their fruits when arrived at maturity. The tasteless seed becomes sweet when it is developed into a stem; and the acid berry of the summer turns saccharine in the harvest. These are the operations of nature, which we sometimes imitate by art. In either case, the internal action, by which the sweetness is produced, has been termed *Saccharification*, and, by some, the *Saccharine fermentation.* The latter denomination has been objected to; but whether or not this change be the consequence of a real fermentation can be judged only when this term is sufficiently defined.

That portion of the flour, or farina, of the cereal grains, and of certain roots, such as potatoes, arrow-root, &c., which forms a turbid milk-like liquid, when mixed with cold water, and is deposited in an almost tasteless powder, is called *fecula.* In its pure state, it is the starch of commerce. It is this fecula that is converted into *sweet* in the incipient process of the vegetation of grain, whe-ther carried on by sowing it in the earth, or by spreading it, in a moist state, on the malting-floor. Bulbous roots, too, become sweet when they begin to spring, as may be generally observed in potatoes, which, in that state, are unfit for culinary purposes.

For the oldest and best-known mode of producing the *saccharification* of barley, or other grain, we must refer our readers to the *Treatise on Malting:* there are other operations that produce a similar effect, which will come more properly under the present head. The artificial saccharification of fruits belongs to the *Treatises on the Brewing of Cyder and Perry,* and on *Wine-Making.*

The discovery of the rapid saccharification of fecula originated with the distillers. " It is thus," says M. Dubrunfaut, " that, in the chemical arts, practice generally precedes theoretical rules; and that the manufacturer, distant from the observations of the learned, is able to produce a certain effect, during a long course of years, before the philosopher has suspected the probability of such a production. In fact, spirituous liquors were distilled from unmalted grain and potatoes, long before the chemical doctrines admitted its possibility.

As soon as the fact attracted their attention, the continental chemists (who more than those of this country apply their science to the arts) endeavoured to elucidate the subject by their experiments. Kirchoff, of St. Petersburg, first converted pure *fecula* into a saccharine semifluid substance, by means of sulphuric acid, with long boiling; and his process, with slight improvements, is still followed by many of the Parisian distillers. This, and other means for effecting the same purpose, are detailed by the author last quoted; but the French distil their materials in a pasty rather than a fluid form, and in such a state, however saccharine it may be, it is unfitted for the brewer. The English and Scotch distillers make pure worts, and these are always capable of being converted into beer. M. Dubrunfaut's method of distilling and brewing from potatoes is worth quoting; being quite practicable, and little known in this country. We shall, however, abridge rather than copy his memoir:—

Having rasped the potatoes as fine

as possible, he put 400 kilogrammes (882 pounds) of the pulp into a brewer's mash-tun, having a double bottom; and while the workmen were stirring the mash in all directions, with oars or rakes, he mixed it with boiling water, which, the *fecula* being set at liberty, turned the whole mass into a jelly, similar to the starch of the laundress. He then added 20 kilogrammes (44 pounds) of malt, ground to a fine powder, and, at the same time, a small quantity of wheat-chaff (*courte paille de froment*) to assist the draining. The whole, being well mixed, began immediately to become fluid, and gradually sweetened, during the space of two hours, when it was drained from the mash-tun in the same manner as is done by the brewer, and carried to the fermenting-tun. A new quantity of liquor was added to the remaining pulp, as a second mash, at the heat of 50° Reaumur (145° Fahrenheit). This being stirred and afterwards drained, the pulp was squeezed in a cylindrical press, in order to get as much of the saccharine as possible, before giving the refuse to the cattle. The liquid fermented well without any deposite that could effect the distillation, and produced 54 litres (14¼ wine gallons) of spirits of the specific gravity .955.

M. Dubrunfaut also applied his discovery to brewing. After having treated the *fecula* in the manner above-mentioned, he added hops, and carried the strength to the specific gravity of 1042, or about 15 pounds per barrel. The wort fermented well, and had a fine vinous smell. It was bottled a few days after, when it ripened, and resembled the beer which is made in Paris. He also fermented the wort without hops, replacing them, as is done in certain provinces, with honey, and obtained a beer which had the taste and other qualities of the famous beer of Louvain.

It will readily be supposed that other farinaceous grains and roots, that is, such as yield a portion, more or less, of starch, may also be converted into saccharine matter; and, in fact, rye, rice, maize, chesnuts, and numerous other mealy fruits, as well as roots, have been made to produce vinous liquors. In this country, however, the chief ingredient, and the cheapest for the purpose, is barley; and to this grain the brewers have, in almost every case, limited their operations. The distillers frequently make use of a mixture of different kinds of grain, and especially oats, but the barley always predominates. We have never seen oats used in the brewery; although it is well ascertained that oatmalt formed one of the ingredients in the multifarious mixture called *mum*, which was a favourite vinous liquor among our ancestors.

The extraction of wort from raw grain was long practised by the Scotch lowland distillers; but it was not until the enormous additions to the malt duties (in 1802 and 1803) that unmalted barley was resorted to by the brewers. From that period until the year 1811, when the practice was checked by the Excise, the more scientific brewers were enabled to save two-thirds of the malt duty; and, consequently, gained an advantage over their less knowing brethren.

Although, by means of a mixture of chaff, a wort may be drawn from raw grain, with the addition of only onetwentieth part of malt, and, we believe, without any malt at all, yet such means have not hitherto been used by the brewer. During an experience of seven or eight years, we found the most convenient proportion to be that of two parts of raw grain to one of malt. The worts, in that case, run more completely from the grains after the first mash. Confined as this usage must now be to private brewings, the quantities must be small, and therefore the following directions are suited to mashes not exceeding three quarters, and at the same time (by observing the proportions), will serve equally well for brewing of half that quantity:—

The malt may be either cut or bruised, but the grain must be cut into very fine meal. The cutting must be sharp, for whatever is powdered into dust is, in a great degree, lost.

Put the quarter of malt, equally spread, on the upper bottom of the mash-tun, and over that the two quarters of cut barley. Introduce into the goods, through the descending trough of the tun formerly mentioned, threefifths of the liquor intended for your first mash (suppose 7½ barrels) at the heat of 155°. In large mashes 150° is sufficient. This liquor rises through the perforations in the false bottom, penetrates the malt, and flows up in fissures through the grain. The goods are then well mashed with oars for half an hour at least. In large quantities it would require, perhaps, twice that time.

The remaining two-fifths (say five barrels) of the intended mash is next to be introduced in the same manner, at the heat of 200°, a few degrees more or less, according to circumstances, and the mashing is to be continued for half or three-quarters of an hour more. The tun is then to be covered and allowed to settle, which may be in an hour. At that time it may happen that a part, if not all, of the worts, will be at the top of the goods, and must be let off through the holes, in the upper part of the trunk at the side of the mash-tun, which we spoke of when describing that utensil. What drains through the false bottom will run off at the same time.

It may be noticed that the reserved portion of the first mash need not be all run on at once. The object is to keep the goods intimately mixed in liquor at an average heat of 140 to 150 degrees, (at which heat the saccharification is more readily obtained,) and for a time sufficiently long to effect that change in every portion of the dissolved fecula. During the whole of the process, the wort increases in sweetness; but neither *taste* nor *time* affords any certainty of the sweetness having reached its maximum. A quantity of unaltered starch may be held in solution, which adds its weight to the liquid, and affects the saccharometer. Although not converted into *saccharum*, it is nevertheless effectual to the distiller, because it undergoes the saccharine fermentation, along with the vinous in the working-tun. It is not, however, the same to the brewer. His endeavour is to stop the attenuation while a portion of the fermentable matter is still weighable in the worts; and it is of some consequence whether that remaining portion be saccharine, or a less altered starch.

The best criterion that has been yet found for ascertaining when the saccharification has reached its last stage, is *iodine*. This substance is a very nice test of the presence of starch, whether in a state of suspension or of solution, in liquids; and, for that purpose, it is used by the continental distillers. If we pour a few drops of the tincture of iodine into a wine glass filled with the worts of raw grain, when the mashing is just begun, the mixture will be instantly coloured of a deep blue. As the saccharification advances, the worts, with the same test, will be lighter and lighter in the tint; until, at last, the colour, remaining unchanged, will show that the transformation of the starch into *saccharum* is completed, as far as this process is effectual for the purpose.

The goods absorb a great proportion of the liquor, so that the worts of the first mash will run very short of what is drawn from malt. The subsequent mash or mashes will present little difference of appearance from those of malted grain; and, in the proportions above stated, will, in most cases, pass freely through the goods in the ordinary way. At all events, the second and third mashes will present no difficulty.

"We should err very much," says Dr. Thomson,[*] "were we to suppose that the whole kernel, or starchy part of the malt is dissolved by the hot water used in brewing. At least one half of the malt still remains after the brewing is over, constituting the grains." "One hundred pounds of malt, from different kinds of grain, after being exhausted as much as usual of the soluble part of the kernel by hot water, were found to weigh as follows:—

English barley . .	50.63 lb.
Scotch barley . .	50.78
Scotch big . . .	52.69

"A hundred pounds of *raw grain* being converted into malt, and the soluble part of the malt extracted by hot water, the residue weighed

English barley . .	51.558 lb.
Scotch barley . .	50.831
Scotch big . . .	53.500

"In another set of experiments, with malt of worse qualities, a hundred pounds of malt left the following residues:

English barley . .	54.9 lb.
Scotch barley . .	56.9
Scotch big	56.6

"It is probable," the Doctor adds, "that an additional portion of the kernel would be dissolved if the malt were ground finer than it is customary to do. The reason for grinding only coarsely is to render it less apt *to set*. But this object might be accomplished equally well by bruising the malt between rollers, which would reduce the starchy part to powder without destroying the husk."

To *bruise* the malt is certainly a preferable practice to cutting it in coarse pieces; but we have been accustomed to grind malt, as well as raw grain, with stones as small as oatmeal, without ever *setting the goods*; and this we con-

* Supplement to th Encyclopædia Britannica; article BREWING.

sider as a still better mode than cylinders, even for malt. In the case of unmalted or badly malted grain the stones are indispensable.

We are perfectly convinced that, in the above-mentioned experiments, the grist must have been either very ill prepared, or the process must have been badly conducted; for a hundred pounds of good malt ought by no means to have left above thirty pounds weight of dry grains.

Raw grain is generally supposed to yield a less proportion of extract than malt; but this, too, we are assured, must be the fault of management. We have before us the results of a number of experiments, on a very large scale, of which the following is an abstract, reduced to a thousand quarters. The grist was barley, oats and malt; the latter in a small proportion—perhaps not more than a twentieth :—

Brewed 8,000 bushels of grain, weighing . . . . 387,300 lbs.
Weight of dry extract, according to Dicas's Saccharometer,
    as nearly as could be ascertained . . . . 253,308 lbs.

Weight supposed remaining in the grains . . . . 133,992 lbs.

Being doubtful, however, of the accuracy of the indications of dry extract by the instrument, a known proportion of the grains was dried, until they had apparently the same dryness as the grain had before grinding; and the weight was found equivalent to fourteen pounds per bushel. The whole of the grains were then measured, and thereby gave another and more accurate comparison. Thus,

Brewed 8,000 bushels of grain, weighing . . . . 387,300 lbs.
Sold   8,672 —— of grains, ditto 121,408

The difference, being the amount of extract 265,892
Dry extract shown by the instrument 253,308

Apparent error in the instrument, being about 5 per cent. . . 12,584

Calculating the proportions from these two sets of experiments :—

	lbs. grain.	lbs. extract.		lbs.
By the first,	100	gave 65.41,	leaving in the grains	34.59
By the second,	100	— 68.65	——	31.35
Average . .	100	— 67.03	——	32.97

It still appears that nearly a third of the kernel remains unextracted; more than half of which, we are convinced, is owing to ignorance of the art. One improvement, in the case now under our consideration, seems obvious: oats, barley, and malt require, each, a different heat for the proper solution of their substance. This might be applied, were each to have its separate mash-tun, but not when they are mingled into one.

Many of the remarks, which we have made in this chapter, may appear to belong to the distillery rather than to the brewery; but the two trades are intimately connected. The distiller and the vinegar-maker are necessarily brewers in the first part of their operations; and, from both, the ordinary brewer may gain instruction. All have this in common, to extract as much of the kernel of the malt, or grain, as they possibly can.

CHAPTER III.

OF THE VINOUS FERMENTATION.

IN whatever way the saccharification is produced,—whether on the malting-floor or in the mash-tun,—the strength of the worts, that is, their power of producing an intoxicating liquid, either in the form of alcohol, or of a vinous liquor, is always accurately designated by the excess of their specific gravity beyond that of water, multiplied by their quantity. Distinct from flavour, this product may be considered as the measure of their comparative value. Thus six barrels of wort, of thirty pounds per barrel, is equivalent to four barrels at forty-five pounds: the product in each case being one hundred and eighty. It has already been shown, in Chapter V. of the first Part, that the extra-weight of a barrel of worts, beyond that of water, is only about four-tenths of the weight of saccharine matter contained in the infusion; but, the proportion being always the same, the weight thus shown by the saccharometer answers all the purposes of the brewer; and it is, therefore, of this extra-weight that the expressions "gravity" and "weight of the wort" are generally understood.

The saccharine extract (or worts) being prepared, and boiled with the hops where that ingredient is required, is next made to undergo the *vinous fermentation*. This chemical process (which was formerly the only change in vegetable extracts that had the name of *fermentation*) operates by the destruction of the *saccharum*, both as to taste and weight; and, when carried to its utmost point, produces a liquid of less specific gravity than water, and of a taste in which the *sweetness* is little, if at all, perceptible: it is *vinous*, or that of wine.

The juices of the sugar-cane, of the grape and of many other fruits, when kept in certain temperatures, enter spontaneously into the vinous fermentation. In the brewing of malt liquors a very general practice has been, to add to the worts a quantity of the *yeast*, or froth of the previous fermentations, in order to hasten the present operation; and it was not until some experiments were made by Mr. Henry, on the effect of carbonic acid, that the chemists conceived that the fermentation of malt liquor could be produced without the assistance of yeast. Notwithstanding, the brewing of ale, without a particle of yeast, has been practised by the farmers of certain districts, in this country, from time immemorial. We have, ourselves, had the experience of worts entering into a spontaneous fermentation, without acquiring any improper flavour, or running into acidity; but they require time, and time cannot be well spared in the modern system of manufactures. What formerly required years to improve must now be brought into the market in two or three weeks. The present mode of porter-brewing is a prominent instance: the large vats, in which that article was wont to be stored for eighteen or twenty-four months, are now comparatively useless.

From the moment that the worts are mixed with the yeast in the fermenting tun, their gravity begins to decrease, and this decrease is termed their *attenuation*. A wort, for instance, of forty pounds per barrel shall, in a few hours, be reduced to ten, by the extrication of carbonic acid, the elements of which must have previously existed in a very condensed state: for, notwithstanding this immense decrease of weight, the quantity, or bulk, of the liquid undergoes no perceptible alteration.

All saccharine liquors, after they have been submitted to the vinous fermentation, are capable of producing a portion of alcohol, by the process of distillation; and the quantity which may thus be extracted is found to be exactly proportionate to the degree of attenuation. Thus a barrel of wort that has lost forty pounds of its weight will produce twice the quantity of pure spirit which could be extracted from a barrel of wort that had lost only twenty pounds in the attenuation. This, too, is independent of the original weight of the wort; for the same extent of attenuation (suppose twenty pounds) will produce the same quantity of spirits, whether the original gravity of the worts has been thirty pounds or fifty.

Seeing that the quantity of spirit is in proportion to the attenuation, it is obviously the interest of the distiller to carry that attenuation as far as possible; and, in as far as alcoholic strength is concerned, this would also be the interest of the brewer. The latter, however, has an additional object in view, namely, *flavour*; and he finds that he cannot please the taste of his customers unless a weighable portion of the saccharum remains in the ale. The former, therefore, is frequently able, by strong fermentations, to reduce his worts to the weight of water, while the latter, after keeping it a twelvemonth, still expects to find from three to six pounds of gravity in his beer. It is for this reason that the brewer is so careful not to exceed in the quantity of yeast which he puts into the gyle-tun; and that, in strong ale, he wishes the tumultuary fermentation in the gyle-tun to close, while eight or ten pounds of the weight still remains unattenuated, to be afterwards slowly decomposed in the casks.

It was long a matter of contest whether alcohol exists ready formed in fermented liquors, or is produced in the process of distillation. The chemists are now generally satisfied that it is produced by the fermentation alone. They have extracted the alcohol at heats far below the boiling point of water, and by other means than by distillation; and, from those experiments, they do not hesitate to assert that alcohol, properly so called, exists in wine and beer. It is not, however, presumed that alcohol is a simple substance; and one who is not a chemist may still suspect that the atoms of which it is afterwards to be composed, although contained in the fluid, may exist in a discordant state, until united by some process that destroys their other affinities. But whatever may become of those theories, it is certain that these atoms, whether separately in solution or combined into alcohol, constitute a *whole* that is lighter than water; for when a wort is fermented so low as to show nothing beyond water, by the saccharometer, it still, according to the experiments of Dr. Thomson, contains about one-fifth of its original saccharum unfermented. Thus a barrel of wort of thirty pounds, when fermented to the weight of water and its alcohol distilled, will leave as much saccharine matter in the still-bottoms, as, if mixed with water to its original quantity, would make a barrel of about six pounds gravity, which might be fermented into beer. This latent weight, or unattenuated gravity, is counterbalanced by the alcohol (or its component parts), which is as much lighter than water as the saccharum is heavier. When ale or beer is attenuated in a great degree, as it usually is when exported to a warm climate, it again enters into a spontaneous fermentation, at the expense of this unattenuated, but latent, saccharum.

The acetous fermentation is the reverse of the vinous. The moment it takes place the vinous liquor becomes heavier by the absorption of oxygen; and the alcohol (or its composing principles) is destroyed, exactly in proportion to the increase of weight. If a distiller's fermenting-tun, for example, shall have been attenuated from the gravity of twenty to that of two pounds, he expects, and would procure, a quantity of spirit corresponding to eighteen pounds of attenuation; but should he, by any oversight, allow the acid fermentation to proceed unobserved, until his worts (wash) should increase in gravity two pounds, so as to show only sixteen pounds of attenuation when they had once shown eighteen, he would find that he had lost the value of two pounds, or exactly one-ninth of the quantity of alcohol which he might have had.

When a distiller's tun has ceased to attenuate, it runs rapidly into the acetous fermentation; and increases in weight at the expense of the alcohol, if (as it is said) the alcohol be really formed. According to this theory, when the attenuation is apparently complete, four fifths of the saccharine matter is converted into equal quantities of carbonic acid and spirit. With a mixture of half that proportion of alcohol, no saccharine liquor would ever become sour. Does

not this circumstance render it probable that the alcohol is not completely formed?

It is so generally allowed, that we have taken it for granted, that the acetous acid (vinegar) is formed, in vinous liquors, by the absorption of oxygen. If this be true, the contact of atmospheric air must be particularly dangerous to the ale-brewer. Various plans have been proposed to prevent its access, but none of them have been successful. In attempting to stop the *acetous*, they check the *vinous* fermentation; and it is only when the latter has completely subsided, that the vessels can be closely bunged up.

Two evils have been stated as the consequence of fermenting worts in open tuns: first, the loss of alcohol, which is supposed to escape in union with the carbonic acid; and second, the germ of acetous acid, which is believed to be communicated to the beer by the contact of the atmospheric air with the surface of the liquid. Patents have been granted, both in France and in this country, for a method of closing the tuns, so as to exclude the atmospheric air, and also to condense any alcohol that may be endeavouring to escape. The plans proposed are of very ancient date, although recently announced as a modern invention of a Mademoiselle Gervais. Our limits do not permit us to describe the particulars; but it is of the less consequence, as we should do so only to show its inutility in the brewery. To those who have seen the pamphlet which circulates the wonderful announcements of the value of the invention, the following remarks will be sufficient: those who have not seen it, may rest satisfied that its perusal would not render them wiser.

Whilst the worts are fermenting, carbonic acid is evolved, and fills a portion of the vacuity of the tun, immediately above the liquor, which excludes the common air as effectually as the closest cover. It can only be when this gas ceases to be generated, that oxygen can gain admittance; and, before that time, every skilful brewer has cleansed his beer into casks, exposing only a small bung-hole, which is also closed the moment the yeast has ceased to issue. During the whole period of the tumultuary fermentation, the pressure is *outward* not *inward;* and a lighted candle, held over the yeasty head, will shew that not a particle of oxygen can be admitted. When this evolution of gas becomes so weak as not to form a stratum above the liquid, the introduction of air may begin, especially if the heat of the tun is high; and this, we believe, frequently happens with the distillers, (who carry the attenuation to the utmost practicable point) especially when the surface of the tun is large in proportion to its depth. A cover in this case is proper, and perhaps it would be better to have an aperture which might be contracted, so as always to preserve a certain depth of stratum of fixed air above the still fermenting liquor.

With respect to the alcohol which is said to be carried off with the carbonic acid, neither can this apply to the brewery, as generally practised. In the heat of a tun which seldom exceeds 75°, the alcohol (or whatever spirituous substance it may be) can lose little or nothing by evaporation. In the Scotch practice, the heat is almost always under 65°; and we know not by what means the particles, that would escape at that temperature, could be condensed. If there really is a loss, it is certainly so small as to be unworthy of attention.

Chapter IV.

Practical Instructions by Mr. Richardson.

Art. I.—For Mild Ale in general.

1.—Heat of the Liquor.

This being an ale which requires early purity, the first heat of the liquor must therefore scarcely ever be under, and is not seldom above, 180°, to which 5° are to be added for the second mash, and 5° more for the third, where three mashes are made for strong ale; but where there are two only, the addition may be 10°; that is, 180° and 190°. If, however, you find by experience that a lower heat of the liquor will produce purity, this will be a preferable practice, as producing a more mucilaginous wort, and it is better calculated for making small beer after it. It is therefore advisable that you begin with the heat of the liquor just mentioned, and then try 175° for the first mash, varying 5° at a time in different brewings, for the sake of practice and experience. Sometimes, indeed, when I take my first heat at 180°, or higher, I only increase 5° for my second, though I have but two mashes for strong ale, in order to avoid

that thinness on the palate, which too high a heat is sometimes apt to produce.

§ 2.—Time of Infusion.

If there be only one mash for strong ale, as is sometimes the case for ale of great strength, the time of infusion should be four hours. If there be two mashes, allow three hours for the first, and two or two and a half hours for the second; and if three mashes, allow two and a half or three hours for the first, two for the second, and one and a half or two hours for the third; it being intended to allow as much time as is consistent with the proper forming of the extract, and the necessary expedition of the process.

§ 3.—Quantity of Hops.

To ale made from worts whose average specific gravity is about thirty pounds (which answers to about two barrels from a quarter of malt), not less than two pounds of hops should be used in winter, and more as the season advances, even to four pounds in a great heat of the atmosphere; or it is perhaps more rational to apportion the hops to the malt used, in which case eight pounds per quarter are allowed, for the more certain preservation of the ale. This being adapted for the climate of England, a greater portion ought to be allowed where the heat of the air is greater.

§ 4.—Time of Boiling.

This in general, should be only till the wort breaks pure, in order to extract only the finer parts of the hops; but in great heats of the air, a longer time in boiling, as well as a greater portion of hops, is necessary for the preservation of the ale. For this purpose, also, (having in view a finer flavour in the ale,) it is advisable to boil the wort for an hour or more, before the hops are added, which renders it more preservable, at the same time that it avoids the rank extract of the hops. If, however, those produced in Worcestershire be used, the mildness of their flavour renders this precaution unnecessary.

What is meant here by *breaking* pure, is that state of the wort when the hops subside to the bottom, and the mucilaginous parts of the malt are coagulated into large lumps, and float up and down in it, very rapidly, leaving the interstices of the wort perfectly pure. This generally happens (when the wort is boiled briskly, as it ought always to be) in about twenty or twenty-five minutes in the first wort, but is somewhat longer in the others. The mode of observing it is, to take a little wort in a bowl or dish, after having boiled about a quarter of an hour, and let it stand steady to observe the effect; and, by doing so every five minutes after, for two or three times, you will note the difference, and soon become a competent judge. Without making this observation, you cannot err much in boiling the first wort about three-quarters of an hour, and an hour or an hour and a half the second; or if you boil altogether, the whole time may be allowed. This, however, respects the extract of the hops rather than the effect it is to have on the wort; and is intended only for the winter season, and when the ale is for present use.

5.—*Method of Fermentation.*

As in this part of the process the greatest effects are produced by the heat of the fermentation, so the greatest attention to its progress is necessary. The first heat (that is, when all the wort is first in the gyle tun) is to be considered of no other consequence than as conducing to the *last* or highest heat to which the fermentation will arrive; and this is found to have a very important influence on the flavour and other qualities of the ale. At 75° the first flavour of mild ale commences; for under that it is more properly the flavour of ale intended to be improved by long keeping. At 80° the flavour of ale is more perfect; at 85° it approaches the *high flavour*; at 90° it may be termed *high*, but is sometimes carried to 100° and upwards; the flavour increasing as the heat of the fermentation rises. It must still be remembered that I refer to the highest heat; and therefore at whatever degree you would have the fermentation finish, you must begin it at such a heat as experience has taught you will rise at last to the desired heat, but no higher. For instance, a wort of thirty pounds per barrel ought to increase about 15°, so that in order to arrive at 80°, you must begin at 65°; but as it is impossible to say how your yeast will ferment (upon the quality of which the success of this operation entirely depends), it were safer in a small gyle, and in a low heat of the atmosphere, to begin at first between 65° and 70°; and if you find it increase 15° or more, you are to lower the heat of your next gyle accordingly;

that is, so as to bring your highest heat of fermentation between 75° and 80°, or not much to exceed the latter; for, though a high heat produces the most agreeable flavour, the ale will not ultimately be so lively, nor will it be so soon fine, as from a contrary practice. It may not, however, be amiss to remark, that Forlow's celebrated Cambridge ale was begun at the heat of 90°, and has been sometimes carried as high as near 110°, producing that peculiarity of flavour which rendered his and the ale at one of the colleges by the same man, so famous, that some of it has been drunk at the king's table.

The quantity of good solid yeast to be used, should be proportioned to the specific gravity of the worts, the prevailing heat of the weather, and the heat of fermentation. To a wort of thirty pounds per barrel, if the heat of the air be low, and the first heat of fermentation 65°, or a little more, two pounds per barrel, or more, may be used. If the first heat be 70°, or not much under, 1½ or 1¾ lbs. may be sufficient. This, when the first heat is about 70°, may be all used at first; when it is lower, two-thirds may be used at first, and the remainder the next morning. In either case the quantity first used should be put into the gyle-tun, and as much wort let down to it as will cover the bottom, one and a half or two inches. The heat of this wort should not be less than 85° or 90°, in which state, being well mixed with the yeast, it puts it into immediate action, and prepares it for the reception of the rest of the wort at the required heat. When an addition of yeast is made, the whole should be well roused, to mix them the more readily.

These previous steps being taken, there is nothing uncertain but the strength and consequent operation of the yeast; and if the heat of the fermentation fall considerably short of the increase before-mentioned, the whole fermentation will be imperfect, the ale will have a heavy mixed flavour of sweet and bitter, and the fault is to be attributed to nothing but want of strength in the yeast. This can only be remedied by a fresh supply from some other brewer; and you must not be disheartened if the first or second change should not succeed; for there must be a new supply procured till some be found which will answer the desired end.

Even when a perfect fermentation is procured, the strength of the yeast will in time degenerate, and render another change necessary; and particularly so when the fermentation is carried to its utmost extent.

It is also to be remembered that I do not recommend rousing the worts in the gyle-tun, except as before-mentioned, because it communicates a rank flavour of yeast to the ale, though it perhaps adds to its strength: this rule, however, can only hold good when the yeast is of sufficient strength; for, when it is weak, or suspected of being so, it will be necessary not only to increase the yeast considerably, by additions at every three or four hours during the day after brewing, but to rouse, at every addition, and even to continue these rousings till cleansing, in order to carry off the saccharine of the malt, and produce, as much as possible, that uniformity of flavour which good yeast would have effected in the first instance.

§ 6.—*Rules for Cleansing.*

It is my practice to look every two hours into the gyle-tun, during the fermentation, whence I observe its progress very accurately. My principal attention is directed to the heat of the fermentation, which generally increases very slowly at first, but when the fermentation is in full force, its general increase is half a degree per hour, which progress declines in proportion as the fermentation advances towards a conclusion, till at length it stands still, and sometimes decreases before the vinous fermentation is entirely complete, especially where the volume of wort is small. This, then, is the grand rule for cleansing: whilst the heat is increasing, you may rest assured that the vinous fermentation is not finished; but so soon as it is at its height, you are to turn your attention to the smell of the ale. Whence you will observe, that in the middle of the fermentation, the fixed air strikes into the head so powerfully, on smelling with the nose lower than the upper edge of the gyle-tun, that it would, perhaps, be death to inhale it a second time, without intermission; but this force so much abates towards the conclusion of the fermentation, that, at the proper period for cleansing, it no longer stings the nostrils, nor strikes violently into the head, but just feels warm, and being drawn into the lungs, only occasions strong efforts to discharge the gas exactly similar to the effect of a sudden exertion in running up a hill, vulgarly termed being *out of breath.* The ale will then have lost its saccharine if the fermentation has been perfect, and will have acquired an uniform vinosity both in its smell and taste. The head will also then have a regular compact appearance of yeast, provided it be so low a heat of fermentation as 75° or a little more, but in proportion as the heat is carried further, the head becomes less; so that a fermentation of 90° or more will only exhibit blistery bubbles, and discharge no yeast till the ale be cleansed into casks, which, in that case, should not be larger than barrels, because it requires the heat to be lessened as expeditiously as may be, to facilitate the discharge of the yeast, and larger casks would be apt to retain it too long.

It is an advisable practice, when the fermentation is carried to its utmost period, to use about seven pounds of flour from either wheat or beans, to a gyle of 25 to 30 barrels, at the time of cleansing, in order to accelerate the discharge of the yeast by the introduction of an extra portion of gas into the ale for that purpose. This should be whisked up in a pail, with some of the ale, till all the lumps are broken, when it may be enlarged to any specific quantity, and then having a portion poured into each cask, agreeably to its size, the ale is to be cleansed upon it.

Though the above rules for cleansing are entirely consistent with my system, I nevertheless have found it convenient to deviate from them, by cleansing at an earlier period, even while the heat of fermentation is yet increasing, and the fixed air is somewhat strong, in order to obtain a better produce of yeast, and thence to have less sediment in the casks, which sometimes subsides with difficulty after removal. By early cleansing, too, the yeast is preserved longer in a state proper for a perfect fermentation, than by a contrary practice. At any rate, however, there must be no saccharine taste perceptible at the time of deciding upon cleansing. When the cleansing is finished, the casks should be filled quite full, and be filled up out of the stillions every two or three hours during the first day, and three or four times the next. When the ale has nearly done its fermentation, if that from the stillions does not run clear, a cask should be tapped, to fill up with, and that which is thick should be returned into the next gyle just before cleansing.

If the ale be racked off from its lees,

about three or four days from cleansing, and you add to every barrel three pints or two quarts of hops, after having boiled in the first wort, and (when the heat of the air is low) whilst they are warm, it will contribute much to the liveliness and purity of the ale, and render it much less liable to disorder, in removing from cellar to cellar; but it is to be observed, that the hops thus added give some rankness to the flavour, and racking is not favourable to the preservation of the ale. In this practice the casks should be filled quite full, and bunged down close, venting only if the cask be in danger. But if the ale be not racked, the casks should not be bunged down so long as the head of the ale can be kept up by repeated fillings; for otherwise there would be a circle of yeast formed round the inside of the bunghole, which would be in part washed off amongst the ale on removal, and tend to make it foul.

CHAPTER V.

Richardson's Instructions continued.

ART. II.—FOR OLD ALE, or such as is to be long kept.

§ 1.—*Heat of the Liquor.*

As purity is not immediately required in this sort of ale, the first mashing heat should be as low as practicable; that is, so as just to avoid acidity in the wort, which is apt to be produced by a very low heat of the liquor. Hence 160° or 165° may be the first heat, and from 10° to 15° may be added for the second, if there be but two mashes, and 10° each if there be three. Thus if the first heat be 160°, and you find no tendency to acidity in the last running of the worts, then these rules may be observed; but if there should be a little acidity discernible, it were advisable to make the increase 4° or 5° more for the subsequent mashes, and on brewing another gyle of the same sort, from the same malt, it were best to begin at 165°, and then observe these rules for the next mashings.

§ 2.—*Time of Infusion.*

If the heat of the liquor be very low, the time of infusion should be somewhat less than that allowed for mild ale. Therefore, two, or two and a half hours may be allowed for the first mash, and one hour for each of the rest.

§ 3.—*Quantity of Hops, and time of boiling.*

The general rule for hops is one pound per bushel of malt; but if it be intended that the ale should retain its mildness to a very distant period (which by the bye is to answer a very useless purpose), a larger portion of hops must be used, agreeably to the intention of the brewer.

The boiling is regulated by time, as the nicety of flavour is not such a requisite in this as in mild ale. In two worts the boiling may be from an hour to an hour and a half for the first, and two or two and a half hours for the second; in three worts, the first may boil one hour, the second an hour and a half, and the last two or two and a half hours.

§ 4.—*Quantity of Yeast, and mode of Fermentation.*

If the first heat of fermentation be not below 60°, and the gravity not much more than thirty pounds, provided the air be temperate, the quantity of yeast must be from two to two and a half pounds per barrel, applied in the manner as directed for mild ale. If the heat be lower, the specific gravity more, or the heat of the atmosphere less, the quantity of yeast must be increased in proportion; in doing of which, no great inconvenience can arise from applying a few pounds too much, but it may occasion an imperfect fermentation if there be a few pounds too little.

The heat of the fermentation should not exceed 75° at the highest, but rest between that and 70°, though the nearer 75° the better will be the flavour of the ale at an early period; and as a low heat of mashing is conducive to a great increase in the heat of fermentation, it will thence be evident that the fermentation for ale, whose average gravity is thirty pounds, must begin at or below 60°, and the precautions before recommended respecting the yeast, must be particularly attended to. The mode of conducting the fermentation, and the criterion for cleansing, being the same with those directed for mild ale, a repetition here would be superfluous.

I, however, recommend a more strict adherence to the rules for cleansing, before inculcated in this process, than in that for mild ale, because the first heat being lower, a greater time is necessary to bring the fermentation to perfection, and secure the future good flavour of the ale. It may be here observed that this sort will generally require finings.

ART. III.—FOR SMALL BEER.

If this be made alone, the same rule is to be observed in the heat of the mashing as that recommended for keeping ale; but the time of infusion is somewhat less. If made after strong ale, as there cannot with propriety be more than one mash, the heat may be 160° or under.

It is generally boiled at once about an hour or an hour and a half, according to the season or the time required to keep it; and it may be observed here, that long boiling prevents its fermenting so freely as it otherwise would do.

The quantity of hops must also depend entirely on the taste of the consumer, and the time required to keep it. When made after mild strong ale, there is generally a sufficient quantity of hops to prevent the necessity of a fresh application, and after keeping ale, the quantity is often so large as to render it necessary to leave some out of it.

The first heat of fermentation may be from 60° to 65°, and, as there is rarely any material increase, it may be cleansed at the end of 12 to 14 hours, when the fermentation is fairly begun; for if it was carried to its utmost period, the beer would be thinner upon the palate, and appear not so strong as it would by the mode of fermentation here recommended.

About a pound of yeast per barrel will be sufficient.

ART. IV.—FOR EARLY HARD ALE, or a mode of producing premature acidity in Ale.

This is nothing more than the artificial introduction of an acid flavour into new ale, to suit particular palates, which flavour must otherwise have been the effect of age. Add to a barrel from one to two gallons of common vinegar, or rather of ale which has acquired a great degree of acid flavour, according to the taste of the consumer whose palate is to be accommodated.

This should be done at such a time as the ale to be changed has discharged the greatest part of the yeast, which may be about twenty-four hours after cleansing, where the heat of fermentation has been low, and from twenty-four to thirty-six hours where it has been high. Some-

times hops are used as in racking of ale. In either case the cask must be filled *nearly full*, and stopped down close, that a violent internal vinous fermentation may ensue, otherwise the union will not be perfect, but the distinct flavours of both will be discernible. If the commotion within seems to endanger the cask by the swelling out of the head, &c., a little of the ale may be drawn off occasionally, but it is to have no other vent.

This fermentation will sometimes continue for three or four weeks, and when it is finished, so that the ale will become pure with finings (which it will require) it will be fit for use.

ART. V.—OF RACKING KEEPING ALE.

Whether the ale be racked from vats or from one cask to another, it has a tendency to grow flat. This may be remedied by adding about two quarts o. hops to a barrel, as mentioned in racking mild ale; but a better mode is by an addition of a sixth to a fourth part of new ale taken from the gyle-tun, in a state proper for cleansing. In either case the cask is to be filled full, and stopped down close, with the same precaution as recommended under the article of *Early hard ale*. I have also seen about a quart of good wort (made perfectly pure by filtrating through a flannel bag) added to a barrel of mild ale, which was flat, but also pure, and, in a very short time, it produced all the liveliness of bottled ale, without having in the least injured its purity; but having had little occasion to pursue the practice, I give it here as a hint well deserving your attention, should you ever have occasion to adopt it.

ART. VI.—FOR BURTON ALE.

This is made from the palest malt and hops; for, if it be not pale as a straw it will not pass with the connoisseurs in that article; and the gravity being so very high as thirty-six to forty pounds a barrel, makes it a matter of great nicety to get malt sufficiently pale.

If the malt be not very good, only one mash must be made for this liquor; but if it be good, two mashes may take place, adverting still to the great specific gravity which ought to be produced.

The heat of the liquor should be 185°, or 190°, adding 5° for the second, if a second mash be made; and the time of infusion may be the same as that mentioned under the article *Mild Ale in general.*

If only one wort be made, it may be boiled an hour and a quarter; if two, they may be boiled three-quarters of an hour the first, and an hour, or an hour and a quarter the second; remembering that long boiling is prejudicial to the colour.

The quantity of hops must be three-quarters of a pound per bushel of malt, or more, according to circumstances; but the more that are used, though an advantage as a preservative, the higher will be the colour of the ale.

The heat of fermentation should not much exceed 75°, and as the first heat would thence probably be about 55°, the quantity of yeast, both on account of this circumstance, and the great weight of the wort, should not be less than three pounds per barrel, used as is before recommended; and the rule for cleansing is the same as that before inculcated.

It is to be racked into clean casks (without hops) when nearly pure, and the sizes of them are from 32 to 42 or 43 gallons (called *half hogsheads*), and from 70 to 80 gallons (called *hogsheads*), which are generally hooped with an equal number of iron and wooden hoops; the latter are white, flat, or broad bark hoops; a bar is put across each head, and the brewer's initials or name, with B or BURTON at length, are branded in front in letters of about an inch and a quarter high; and the number of gallons which the cask holds is cut with a scribe-iron, just above the cork-hole.

The bung-hole is not above an inch and a quarter diameter, which is stopped with a wooden shive or bung, and a piece of triangular tin-plate is afterwards nailed over it.

CHAPTER VI.

Richardson's Instructions continued.

ART. VII.—FOR PORTER.

§ 1.—*Heat of the Liquor.*

The heat of the liquor may begin from 156° to 165°, it being intended to go as low as the avoiding acidity in the wort will admit of; and, as a large portion of the malt in this is brown, the heat of the liquor may thence be, with safety, somewhat lower than in the process of keeping ale.

The subsequent heats of the mashes are to be increased from 5° to 10° each, according to circumstances, though the former is generally sufficient. If, however, the ranker earthy parts of the malt be desired, in order to heighten the flavour; or if the taste of the preceding wort has been somewhat inclined to acidity, then 15° may be added, supposing a very low beginning.

§ 2.—*Time of Infusion.*

This, on account of the number of mashes, need not be more than two hours at the first, and one hour for each of the rest; but as the time of boiling allows more time between the two last mashes than usual, the time of infusion may be proportionately long, without wasting any.

§ 3.—*Quantity of Hops, and Time of Boiling.*

It is not, perhaps, so much for the purpose of preservation as for that of flavour, that the general practice is to use not less than four, and sometimes four and a half to five pounds per barrel for *keeping;* though what is termed *mild* or *mixing* porter, has not more than three to three and a half pounds; but since hops have been so very dear, these proportions have been so considerably lessened, that I do not even now use more than three and a half pounds for *keeping.*

The hops required here are to be *strong,* without regard to colour; and for the purposes of extracting all that strength, and communicating all its rankness, the whole of the worts are generally boiled from eight to nine hours in the aggregate; which may be apportioned, in three worts, to one and a half, two and a half, and four or five hours. If there are four worts, it may be one, one and a half, two and a half, and three or four hours.

§ 4.—*Mode of Fermentation.*

The heat of fermentation to be so low as not to exceed 70° when at the highest, so that in general it may begin about 60°; and should it be inclined to go further than 70°, provided the saccharine of the malt be not perfectly gone off, the event of a degree or two more may be waited for, in case the heat of the fermentation does not increase more than half a degree in the hour at that time, when it is to be cleansed at all events; otherwise, it might run up so high as to induce the flavour of keeping ale instead of that fulness which porter ought to have. If, when the heat of fermentation is at 70°, it is increasing more than is above mentioned, I recommend that the porter be cleansed, lest the major part of the yeast subside to the bottom of the casks instead of being thrown out, and thence render the porter foul, and hereafter stubborn, if not cloudy. At this period of the fermentation, though every other rule relative to cleansing be dispensed with, yet care should be taken that the sweetness of the malt be gone off; and to facilitate that end, a greater portion of yeast is to be used than is allowable in any other beer of the same strength. The quantity required is from three to four pounds per barrel, used in the usual proportions, and rousing the wort every two hours in the day time, and even during cleansing, if practicable, in order to give every degree of rankness obtainable from the materials.

In order to heighten the flavour, about a quarter to half an ounce of socotrine aloes per barrel may be boiled in the second wort; and, for the purpose of giving a retentive head, as much salt of steel as will lie on a half-crown piece is to be added to a barrel, with the finings. These effects may, indeed, be increased to any desired degree, by increasing the quantity; but it is to be remembered that aloes is a powerful purgative, and much more than half an ounce per barrel might discover itself, nor is the salt of steel sufficiently wholesome to warrant the use of any large quantity. The former of these I now entirely omit, and in its place use quassia, in the proportion of a pound to twenty barrels of porter, or a little less; and, as a saving, copperas may be substituted in the place of the latter.

The malt used is generally brown, amber, and pale, in equal quantities; but it is necessary, in that case, to have the former browner than is always to be met with; and the second of a deeper tinge; it may be as well to use brown and pale in equal parts, or in such other proportions as the colour of the former shall indicate to be necessary even to two-thirds or more: and, as it is essential, both for colour and flavour, to have a sufficient portion of brown, an error on that side would be much more safe than on the other; for the want of colour, and consequently of flavour, is often a great obstacle to the reception of porter, in a country where its production is novel, by rendering it more like

ale than is admissible in such a situation; where it is generally expected to find in it qualities which, in the known produce of London, would not, perhaps, be demanded.

The malt, both brown and amber, are dried with wood, either billets or very stout faggots; but this being for the sake of flavour only, where there is a deficiency of this fuel, the foundation or body of the heat may be produced and continued with cinders, adding some wood.

When the porter is worked off, it should be started into vats, of any convenient size, from 50 to 500 barrels, and racked thence for sending out; in doing which it is preferable to rack the whole off at once, that there may be no ullage, which is apt to become vapid and often sour. It should not be racked till on the fret.

§ 5.—*Of the average Specific Gravity requisite for different Ales and Porter.*

For Burton ale, as is before intimated, the first sort is from forty to forty-two, or forty-three; the second from thirty-five to forty; and a third sort, made after the former, is from twenty-eight to thirty-two, or thirty-three pounds per barrel.

This latter is the usual gravity for common mild strong ale, of the first quality; but the more prevailing weight for common ale is from twenty-five to twenty-seven; and even since malt became so valuable, from twenty-two to twenty-four is deemed sufficient; whilst in certain situations twenty to twenty-one is thought to be as much as the price merits.

For keeping ale which is similar to the above, only in being longer kept before used, the same gravities are requisite.

For porter, about eighteen is sufficient for the common sort, twenty for what is sometimes termed *double;* twenty-two to twenty-three for the first kind of brown stout, and twenty-five to twenty-six pounds for the very best brown stout.

The weight for common small beer is about six or seven; and what is deemed good table beer, is from twelve to fourteen pounds.

ART. VIII.—OF RETURNS *for saving Malt.*

After the usual process of brewing is finished, you are to cause one or two mashes to be made, according to circumstances ; viz. if small beer has been made, only one mash is to take place ; but where that has not been the case, there may be two ; for the more the malt is exhausted, the greater is the saving, and the greater the number of mashes, the more fermentable matter is extracted.

If, therefore, no small beer is intended to be made, you are to mash for a return in the same manner as if small beer was to be made, only using as much more liquor as is convenient ; taking the heat at 160° or 165°, letting it infuse an hour or more, and then pumping it up into the copper, and putting the hops into it, but it is only to be just made to boil when it is to be turned into the cooler in the usual way. During this another mash for a second return is to be made, taking the heat at 5° lower than the first, which return being pumped up into the copper, and the hops added to it, it may remain in the copper all night at a heat nearly boiling, and then be turned into the cooler as the former.

These two returns are to remain in the coolers until the evening before the next brewing, when they are to be let down into the under back and pumped into the copper, to serve for the purpose of mashing, in the place of so much liquor ; and if there be more than sufficient for the first mash, the remainder may have as much liquor added to it as will serve for the second. But as the return contains a certain portion of fermentable matter, that portion is to be previously ascertained, and either an additional quantity of liquor is to be used in the brewing, or so much malt be left out of the grist as the amount of that fermentable matter may be.

To ascertain this, it may be premised that the gravity of the wort intended for small beer is generally from three to five, more or less, and that the wort drawn after this (if the quantity be the same as that of the wort for small beer) will have half, or rather more than half the weight of that ; so that supposing the gravity of the wort for small beer to have been 3.5, the wort intended for a return would probably be 2.0 ; in which case, if the volume of the wort amount to twenty barrels, the sum would be forty pounds, or upwards of half a quarter of malt. On the contrary, if no small beer be made, the

mash which would have been made for that wort must now be made for a first return, to which another mash, as above mentioned, would produce a second, whence the saving would be nearly threefold of the one effected after making small beer ; for, supposing twenty barrels of the first return at 3.5, the aggregate would be seventy pounds, to which the second return (as above estimated) being added, the total would be one hundred and ten pounds, or nearly one quarter and a half of malt, valued at seventy-five pounds per quarter.

But as this estimate only relates to the return in the under back, it is to be remembered that an addition would be made to the amount, as exhibited in that state, by that portion of the preceding worts which is imbibed by the hops, and which will be extracted and replaced by the return into which those hops are put ; but this addition can only be ascertained by actual experiment. Whence *the net aggregate saving is to be estimated from the gravity of the return taken when cold in the cooler*, as including the above-mentioned addition from the hops, and not from the return in the under back, the aggregate of which will be found to fall considerably short of that of the return in the coolers, particularly where many hops are used.

There is also some advantage derived from the hops having their virtue further extracted by this process ; but as an estimate of the *quantum* cannot easily be made, it is not taken into the account of the saving effected hereby.

The intervention of a day or two between the brewings is no bar to the use of a return. Its very humble specific gravity is a security against fermentation. In summer we sometimes have it lie a week ; and, in very warm weather, it will mould a little at the top without injuring its taste. I do not, however, use it for strong ale in such cases, but mash with it for another return, that the flavour and purity of the former may not be affected by it ; but for porter I never hesitate to use it at first, and we generally contrive to brew a gyle of the latter after one of the former, with that intention.

ART. IX.—OF THE BREWING BOOK.

The following is the plan of my brewing book :—

BREWING- BOOK.

1	2	3	4	5	6	7	8	9	10	11	12	13	14		15	16	17	18	19		20
1800	Malt.	Hops.	H. Liq.	Liq.	Wrts.	Grav.	Sum.	Boil	Worts.	Grav.	Sum	Yeast.	Heat of Fer.		Hours.	X.	P.	T.	Fermentation.		Remarks.
12.8	12	48	170	24	14	32.8	452	1	10	38.0	380	40	74½	11½	36				Time.	Heat	
X & T	(76)		175	14	14	18.0	248	1½	11½	23.0	264								8 E. 7	74½	
No. 16			180	14	14	9.5	131	2½	9½	14.0	133								9 M. 8	79	
																			— 10	80	
				52	42		831		31	25	777								— 12	80⅞	1½ O. P.
																			E. 3	81⅞	
			165	15	15	5.4	80	1	12	7.5	90	12	66	1	12	31		12	— 5	82½	
																(25)		(7.5)	10 M. 8	86	
							911				867										
12.11	12	108	150	26	16	28.2	444	1	12	32.5	390	140	66	7	33				12 M. 4	66	
P	(75)		155	15	15	15.6	231	1½	12½	18.0	225								— 9	66½	
½.0.6½			160	15	15	9.5	140	2½	13½	12.0	162								— E. 1	66½	
No. 17			165	16	16	5.4	85	3	12	8.0	96								— 5	67½	2 Q.
																	50		13 M. 9	72	
																	(17.5)		— 11	72½	
				72	62		900		50		873								E. 1	73	
	24	156	Carried over.													31	50	12			

EXPLANATION.

Suppose the Book lying open, as in the two pages * before us, both of which are to be taken across as continued lines of the same Table:—

Column 1, contains the date and quality of each brewing as successively numbered No. 1, No. 2, &c., from the beginning of the year, which is here counted from the 1st of October. The two examples are reductions of two of my own brewings for twelve quarters. Herein 12.8 means December 8th; X and T are strong beer and small; P is porter; and the figures $5\frac{1}{4}.0.6\frac{1}{2}$ denote $5\frac{1}{4}$ quarters of brown malt, no amber, and $6\frac{1}{2}$ quarters of pale. Column 2 shows the quarters of malt used, and col. 3 the pounds of hops, both of which are summed up at the bottom of every page, so as to show the quantity used at the close of the year. Col. 4 is the heats of liquor for each mash; and col. 5 is the barrels of liquor. Col. 6 is the quantity of worts drawn from each mash; col. 7 is the gravity per barrel taken in the underback; and col. 8 is the whole weight of fermentable matter, deducting one and a half per cent. for heat. Col. 9 gives the hours each wort is boiled. Col. 10 gives the worts in the coolers; col. 11 their gravity; and col. 12 the sum of the gravities multiplied by the quantities. Col. 13 shows the pounds of yeast. The double column 14 gives the first heat of fermentation, and its increase in the gyle-tun; and col. 15 shows the hours which it remains in the tun before cleansing. Columns 16, 17, and 18 show the quantities of strong ale, porter, and table beer brewed; and these, like those of the malt and hops, are summed up on each page, and carried forward to the succeeding one.

The next column contains minutes of the progress of the *fermentation*. Thus, in the first example, 8 Ev. 7—$74\frac{1}{2}$ shows that the yeast was put to the worts, at $74\frac{1}{2}$ degrees of heat, on the 8th of December, at 7 o'clock in the evening. Its progress through the next day is marked in the same manner; and on the 10th, at 8 in the morning, the ale appears to have been cleansed; having acquired an increase of $11\frac{1}{4}°$ of heat in the course of thirty-six hours.

The last column or space is left for remarks. Those here inserted signify

* On two pages in the Manuscript, but here printed on one.—EDIT.

$1\frac{1}{2}$ pound of orange peas, and 2 pounds of quassia.

The figures in column second, marked with *red ink*, [here within parentheses] (76) and (75) is the produce per quarter, as shown by the saccharometer. The same sort of figures in columns 16, 17, and 18 give the weight per barrel of the different beers.

With respect to the high fermentation mentioned when speaking of Cambridge ale, Mr. Richardson has given no examples; and our practice, in this kind, has been so limited, that we can only exhibit a single brewing, on the results of which we can depend. This was a brewing of eight quarters of malt, with forty pounds of hops. It immediately followed one from which there was a Return of eighteen barrels, of four pounds specific gravity, which was made use of for the first mash. It was in the month of February, and the weather was uncommonly mild.

	Barrels.		lbs.
1st Mash 18	gave 11	at 34	= 374
2d Mash 10	10	- 20	= 200
3d Mash 10	10	- 10.5	= 105
	31		679
Return 16	16	- 3.	= 48

The three worts when boiled produced $22\frac{1}{2}$ barrels at 29 lbs. per barrel; and this with the Return (which infused with the hops showed 15 barrels at 4 lbs. per barrel) gave a produce; on the whole, equal to eighty pounds per quarter.

These $22\frac{1}{2}$ barrels were pitched at 78° with four gallons of yeast. In thirty-six hours the heat rose to 94°, when it was cleansed at 14 lb. gravity. In about a fortnight it was pure, and turned out to be excellent ale.

CHAPTER VII.

OF THE LONDON BREWERY.

WHILE the character of the London ale is so low as to be unknown beyond the precincts of the metropolis, that of the porter remains unrivalled. Tastes are acquired by habit, from which cause, when in continued action, we get inured to the strangest beverage. The immense capitals and influence of the ten or twelve principal houses defy all competition, and whatever malt liquor they may agree to designate by the name of porter must, eventually, pass current with the multitude. This is no random assertion; for it is well known that the liquor now retailed under that denomination has little or no resemblance to what was so called thirty years ago. Whether it is better or worse, or whether there can now be any criterion of comparison, in that respect, is no part of the question.

"Before the year 1730, the malt liquors in general use in London were ale, beer, and twopenny, and it was customary for the drinkers of malt liquor to call for a pint, or tankard, of half-and-half, that is, a half of ale and half of beer, a half of ale, and half of twopenny, or half of beer and half of twopenny. In course of time it also became the practice to call for a pint, or tankard, of *three threads*, meaning a third of ale, of beer, and of twopenny; and thus the publican had the trouble to go to three casks, and turn three cocks, for a pint of liquor. To avoid this inconvenience and waste, a brewer of the name of Harwood conceived the idea of making a liquor which should partake of the same united flavours of ale, beer, and twopenny. He did so, and succeeded, calling it *entire*, or entire-butt; and, as it was a very hearty and nourishing liquor, it was very suitable for *porters* and other working people: hence it obtained the name of PORTER."

It is not to be recorded in honour of the chemical arts, but it is nevertheless true, that many of the now indispensable ingredients and manipulations originated in the wish to deceive. It was early known that what was then termed the *fiery* nature of newly distilled spirits became softened by long keeping, but it was found, at the same time, that when, as was usually the case, they were kept in oak casks, the liquor acquired a brown tinge, more or less deep, according to the time of maceration; and hence, with the unobservant purchaser, colour was taken for the criterion of age. This error, however, is now exploded; and every one knows that rum and brandy owe their beauty to artificial infusions. In a similar manner, all other things alike, ale and beer assume a lighter or a deeper dye in proportion to the quantity of malt-extract which they contain; because malt, however carefully dried, always acquires some degree of colour from the kiln. Colour, therefore, with the many, was long considered as indicative of strength.

The manufacture of fine ales (before they were contaminated with hops) was intended to imitate the white wines of the continent; and, consequently, in those times, the paler the malt the more valuable it was, in that respect, to the ale-brewer. Nevertheless, when the quantity of malt was great, the worts were always partially coloured; and the produce being termed "strong or *mightie* ale," induced the public brewer to make two beverages from the same malt of equal strength but of different colours, until at last *paleness* was gradually disregarded. In the case of beer, which contained numerous ingredients, the quality of the malt was less attended to. The harvesting of barley was then more troublesome than now, and much of it was moulded and stained. To hide these defects in the malting, it was coloured on the kiln, and hence the early manufacture of brown malts, which were sold only to make beer. Brown malt always smells of the fire; and this empyreumatic flavour, becoming in request, was heightened by drying with wood faggots, chiefly beech, because that sort of wood was formerly of little value. Thus did beer acquire a deep colour; and when hops were introduced, and subsequently enforced by legal enactments, the bitter principle being all that was sought for, the brownness of colour and the coarseness of the flavour formed no objection to their use.

When the saccharometer was applied to the brewery, it was discovered that the colouring matter of brown and amber malts was formed at the expense of the *saccharum;* and this added to the knowledge that these sorts of malt were made from barley which was unfitted for the paler kinds, rendered it desirable to find substitutes for flavour and colour from other substances. The sale of colouring was at first private, but being authorized to be made from sugar by the 51 Geo. III., it became a trade; and, under cover of that article, other ingredients were sometimes introduced which were neither legal nor useful.

In 1816, all ingredients, other than malt and hops, were forbidden, and consequently the manufacture of sugar-colouring was discontinued; but in a short time after, a patent was taken out for the making of colouring by the roasting of malt: and this colour, being legal, is made use of by those brewers who prefer it to the old mixture of brown and amber. When this roasted malt is put into the mash-tun, all the rest of the malt is pale; and the proportion of black to pale is about one to forty or fifty, according to the degree of colour required.

Whether it is produced from brown, amber or black malt, from burnt sugar or burnt molasses, the colouring principle is the same. The flavour, however, may be, and, we believe, is, different. In either case the colour is produced by the roasting of *saccharum;* but as the whole of the malt is not *saccharum*, the roasting to blackness mixes the colouring part with a large proportion, probably a half, of common charcoal. The charcoal will, no doubt, subside, but its previous effects are unknown, and, accordingly, some of the principal brewers have never used black malt; and none of them, we believe, brew either their keeping porter or their brown stout without the admixture of brown or amber malt. Private families may colour and flavour as they please; and we are persuaded that, in making porter, they will find the charring of sugar the most convenient. For this purpose a quantity of brown sugar, moistened with water, may be put in a frying-pan, the bottom of which should be covered to about an inch deep. This is then to be roasted on a fire, and stirred for some time, until it inflame spontaneously. The flame, after it is judged (from practice) to have burnt long enough, is then extinguished by a cover; and water is added to the pitch-like residue until the whole has the consistence of treacle, when it is put into a bottle or can for use. This colouring is afterwards to be mixed with the worts in the copper in such quantities as are required.

Mr. Richardson's instructions for the brewing of porter, if literally followed, would produce a clean and full-tasted liquor; but they are deficient in some particulars, with respect to the after-management, especially in the London practice. It may be here noticed, by the way, that the quassia, or aloes, which he recommends cannot be used with impunity; and, therefore, the quality and quantity of the hops are now more strictly attended to than in former times. The gravity, too, differs much from his example; for we believe that there is seldom any gyle now made of a less weight than twenty pounds. We may add that the heat of the tun is now less attended to. The criterion for cleansing is the attenuation; and when that has sunk to ten or eleven pounds, (which is usually in less than forty-eight hours)

the operation is begun. By this time the heat is generally about 75°, being pitched at 65°; and a degree of heat, in a good fermentation, usually accompanies a degree of attenuation.

About five-and-twenty years ago, when we first attended to the brewing of London porter, it was the practice to keep very large stocks of that article for twelve or eighteen months; for the purpose, as was then thought, of improving its quality. The beer was pumped, immediately after it was cleansed, into store-vats, holding from five to twenty gyles (brewings) each. The usual size was between four and six thousand barrels; but one, the boast of its brewhouse, contained eighteen thousand, and was said to have cost ten thousand pounds. The porter, during its long repose in those vats, became spontaneously fine, and, by a silent fermentation, lost the greater part of its remaining saccharum. Its bitter, also, grew less perceptible, and the liquor was transformed into *good, hard* beer. This was softened by the publican to the taste of the customer, by the addition of such as was *mild*, that is, newly brewed; but little of this milder sort was at that time required. The taste of the metropolis has since undergone a great change; so much so, that more than half of all that is brewed is drunk before it is six weeks old. The demand for mild beer is still increasing; and we cannot better detail its progress, and explain the nature of the mixtures of *mild* and *stale*, than by copying the information given by Mr Barclay (of the firm of Barclay, Perkins, and Co.) to the Committee of the House of Commons, in the year 1818:—

"What quantity of beer do you now brew annually?—About 300,000 barrels.

"Is sour or stale beer used in your vats with new beer, to your knowledge? —To answer the question correctly, I should state, that every publican has two sorts of beer sent to him, and he orders a proportion of each as he wants them; the one is called *mild* beer, which is beer brewed and sent out exactly as it is brewed; the other is called *entire*, and that beer consists of some brewed expressly for the purpose of keeping: it likewise contains a proportion of returns from publicans; likewise the beer which we receive from public-houses, which has been brewed by other brewers, and which have changed into our trade (as it is our plan always to clear the cellar of a publican before he begins to draw our beer); and likewise a portion of the beer the bottoms of vats; the beer that is drawn off from the pipes which convey the beer from one vat to another, and from one part of the premises to another; this beer is collected and put into vats: it also contains a certain portion of *brown stout*, which is twenty shillings a barrel dearer than common beer: it also contains some bottling beer, which is ten shillings a barrel dearer. I should observe, that the beer returned from the publican is always examined by a class of clerks called coopers, and, as far as they can possibly judge, if there is any admixture of any kind or sort, if it has been weakened, it is put aside, and in some instances been thrown away, and the person not allowed for it; but, in general, there is an examination made of the beer upon being returned. Now all these beers united are put into vats; and it depends upon various circumstances how long they may remain in those vats before they become perfectly bright; when it becomes bright it is sent out to the publicans for their *entire* beer, and there is sometimes a small quantity of mild beer mixed with it.

"Do you ever buy *sour* or *stale* beer of any other persons than the publicans whom you serve?—The Committee will observe by my preceding answer that the publicans require a certain quantity of this stale beer, which they mix with the mild beer, according to the taste of their customers, some preferring it new, and some older; but I should observe, that the taste of the town is continually changing, so that now they use but very little of this entire beer; and if the trade of a brewer increases very rapidly, he may not have sufficient stale beer of his own to send to his publicans, and that was the case with our house some years back; and I believe since, in two or three instances. Upon those occasions we have bought stale beer of other brewers, but in doing that we have been extremely careful in selecting only that of the best quality.

"Is that stale beer *sour* beer?—That beer has not got the acetous fermentation upon it; if it had it would not be fit for use. It is what is commonly called *hard beer*.

"You have stated that there are a number of beers mixed together; have you any fixed proportion in that mixture?—It is the remnants of everything; and I have described to the Committee

what it consists of, and that a part of those remnants are of a very superior quality, particularly when they come to the bottom of the brown stout.

"What proportion of the whole number of barrels sent out would those remnants form?—About one tenth: we send out about one tenth of entire, but that is not consisting of remnants, because, I believe I stated before, that part of it is beer brewed and kept for that purpose.

"What proportion might the remnants form of the whole 300,000 barrels?—Our return is about 10,000 barrels a year, which includes beer brewed by other brewers, and which have been taken of publicans who have come into our trade, a good deal of which is mild beer.

"Is the beer that is composed of remnants wholesome and good liquor?—Perfectly so.

"Is it absolutely necessary that a publican should have some of these remnants to mix it for the taste of his customers?—I should think so. It has been the constant practice as long as I have known the trade; and in former years they used to draw more of that *entire* than they do now.

"Is not that *hard* or *stale* beer mixed to give the porter the appearance of age at once, which formerly was allowed to be matured by time?—It must have the effect of making the beer taste older; but I should think that the beer which was formerly kept a twelvemonth would not be drank by the public; their taste is for mild beer.

"Does the use of stale beer effect a quick sale in the trade, and consequently a quicker return?—I do not see how the publican could well please his customers unless he had the means of making his beer either stale or mild as they wish for it. The Committee will see that if the brewer had not this vent for selling his *return-beer*, the price of beer must be considerably higher if he is to throw this beer away, which amounts altogether to near 20,000 barrels in our house alone."

CHAPTER VIII.

OF SCOTCH ALE.

THE distinguishing characteristics of Scotch ale, are paleness of colour, and mildness of flavour. The taste of the hop never predominates, neither in its stead do we discover that of any other ingredient. It is perhaps more near to the French pale wines, than any of the other ales that are brewed in this country. Like them, too, it is the result of a lengthened fermentation.

The low heat at which the tun is pitched, confines the brewing of Scotch ale to the colder part of the year. During four or five of the summer months, the work (except perhaps in some houses for table beer) is completely at a stand, the utensils are limed down, and the greater part of the workmen discharged. No strong ale is either brewed or delivered.

The Edinburgh brewer is particularly nice in the choice of his malt and hops. The former is generally either English, or of his own making from English barley; and the latter Farnham, the finest East Kent, or a mixture of both. The yeast (or *store*, as it is termed) is carefully preserved, and measured into the gyle-tun, in the proportion of about three gallons to twenty barrels of wort.

The Scotch practice is to take only one mash, and that pretty stiff, for strong ale, making up the quantity of wort (*length*) by eight or ten subsequent sprinklings of liquor over the goods, which are termed *Sparges*. These sparges trickle successively through the goods, and wash out as much more of the saccharine from the mash, as may suffice for the intended strength of the ale. In this manner, specific gravities may be obtained much higher than could be done by a second mash, which always requires a certain portion of liquor before the goods can be made sufficiently fluid. If we suppose this necessary portion of liquid in a particular mash to be fifteen barrels, it would be found, on trial, that these fifteen barrels, when drawn from the mash-tun, would not contain nearly so much saccharine matter as might have been extracted by ten successive sparges of a barrel each. The reason of this will be obvious, if we recollect that the grains always remain wetted with wort equivalent in strength to that of the wort last drawn off, and that the quantity remaining on the goods is about three-fourths of a barrel to a quarter of malt. The gravity of this imbibed wort will, in the one case, be equal to that of the second mash; but in the other, will be reduced to that of the tenth sparge, or washing. Mr. Richardson, so often quoted, condemns this practice; but, in doing so, we know that he labours

under a mistake. "What power," says he, "or what time, has a fluid to extract, which is sprinkled over the surface of the materials, and immediately trickles out below, without being allowed a stationary moment for *infusion ?*" We answer, that in malt (and it is only of malt brewings that we now speak) the *infusion*, if properly conducted, is finished with the *first mash*; and that nothing more is necessary than to draw out from the goods, in a pure state, that saccharine matter which the first infusion has set free. But the question with us does not depend on theory. We have brewed strong ale for years, without following it either with table beer or returns, and we have, in all cases, drawn as much from the malt as we could have done by repeated mashings. The only objection to the *sparging system* is the loss of time.

The first part of the process is to mash with liquor heated to 180° at least,* and generally to 190°, varying with the dampness of the malt. According to Dr. Thomson, the best brewers take the lower heats, but this is doubtful. After mashing from twenty minutes to half an hour, that is, until every particle of the malt is in contact with the liquor, the tun is covered, and the whole allowed to *infuse* about three hours, when it is drained off into the under back, or (what is far better) into the wort copper.

After the first wort is run off, a quantity of liquor (generally a barrel), at the heat of 180°, is sprinkled equally over the surface of the goods. To prevent the liquor from dashing on one part, it is usually received upon a circular board, about three feet diameter, which is swung over the centre of the mash-tun; and, being perforated with small holes, allows the water to descend in a shower. The board being hung on cords, is moveable by the hand over every part of the surface of the tun. When, as generally happens, the cock of the liquor-copper is not high enough to carry the liquor to the board, a separate cock is inserted in the side for that use only. Other means may be adopted to answer this purpose of sprinkling, the object being to spread the liquor, equably, in a shower over the whole surface of the goods, as if from the rose of a watering-pan.

When the barrel (or other quantity)

* It is here to be observed that we merely record the practice: not our own opinion of its propriety

of liquor is thus let in upon the goods, the cock of the mash-tun is opened, so as to let it off, as in the case of an ordinary mash. Some brewers, instead of the common outlet of the mash-tun, have three or four small cocks inserted in different parts of the bottom, from the fear that a single cock might draw the filtrating liquor to one point, and thereby create a crack in the goods, instead of leaving the whole of the liquor to descend in one horizontal stratum.

When the first sparge is run off, or nearly so, which may be in twenty or five and twenty minutes, another of equal quantity is put on the goods, in the same manner, and thus, successively, until the whole of the sparges, when mixed with the first mash worts, show that gravity which is desired. The strong ale worts are then completed, and a mash is made to search the goods either for table beer, or a return, as the trade requires. This mash, however, is not necessary as a saving of extract ; for the whole of the saccharine matter of the malt may be exhausted, as well as any required gravity of wort produced, by means of sparges alone ; but there is an opinion, probably not ill founded, that the last weak extracts are less fitted for fine ale. The making up of strengths from the coolers formerly explained, is here anticipated, being regulated by the saccharometer in the under back, or wort-copper ; for practice soon teaches the increase that is produced by the boiling. It may be here noticed, that after the first sparge at 180°, it is customary with some brewers to reduce the others gradually, so that the last is perhaps 175° or 170°.

All rankness of flavour being carefully avoided in this species of ale, the quantity of hops seldom exceeds four pounds to the quarter of malt ; and the bitter thus created being too slight to cover the taste of ruder ingredients, we believe that the Edinburgh brewers have been less the prey of travelling druggists than their brethren of the south. A little honey to add to the sweet, and a few coriander seeds or other aromatics to assist the flavour, are, as far as we have learnt, the amount of the sins of which they have been accused.

The manner of boiling the worts does not differ from the directions of Mr. Richardson ; but when they arrive at the gyle-tun, the process of brewing is no longer the same. The first heat of fermentation, in the Scotch method, is as low as possible, consistent with the action. The favourite heat is 50°, a point at which chemists have generally asserted that the vinous fermentation could not exist, but 45° and 46° are by no means uncommon in the manuscript brewing-books that now lie before us. Even in the coldest weather, the lowness of heat is not to be feared, provided the brewery be in full work. The fermentation sometimes continues for three weeks, and a fortnight would be a pretty fair average. Were the brewings made three times a week, seven or eight working-tuns would thus be generally in play ; and these being in the same room, some of them at 12 or 15° of increased heat, would create an atmosphere for themselves.

The quantity of yeast formerly mentioned is generally sufficient, but, in some cases, an addition is made a day or two after, if, in the judgment of the brewer, it appears necessary. The least quantity that will carry forward the fermentation to the required point is always preferred ; and, to assure that purpose, the tun is roused twice a day (morning and evening) to prevent its becoming too languid. This rousing is continued until the ale is nearly ready for cleansing.

The rule for cleansing differs from that given by Mr. Richardson. It is an application of his saccharometer, of which he himself was not aware. The attenuation is attended to daily, and, towards the close of the operation, twice a day. While the heat is increasing, the attenuation proceeds ; that is, the weight of the worts continues to diminish. After a certain time, the heat has reached its highest point, and begins to lessen. It is here that we are directed by Mr. Richardson to trust to the *smell ;* but this *smell* merely informs us that carbonic acid continues to be evolved, and the same circumstance is, in consequence, indicated by the saccharometer : for as long as any such evolution of gas exists, so long will the weight of the worts continue to diminish. When the progress of the attenuation is so slow as not to exceed half a pound in twenty-four hours, it is prudent to cleanse, especially if the attenuation is already low ; for it might otherwise happen, that the gas being too weak to buoy up the now close head of the tun, the yeast might partially or wholly subside, and the ale would become *yeast- bitten :* it would receive that disagreeable taste which the head had acquired by too long exposure to the atmospheric air.

When the ale is cleansed, the head, which has not been disturbed for two or three days, continues to float on the surface, till the whole of the *then* nearly pure liquid is drawn off into the casks; and this is considered as a preservative against the admission of the atmospheric air: for the Scotch do not skim their tuns as the London ale brewers so generally do. The ale thus cleansed does not require to be placed on close stillions. It throws off little or no yeast, and a tub placed so as to catch any little overflow of the scum that arises is quite sufficient. The fermentation is almost finished in the tun; and it is not the wish of the brewer that it should proceed much farther.

The strength of Scotch ale, when it deserves the name, ranges between thirty-two and forty-four pounds weight to the imperial barrel, that is, of a specific gravity between 1089 and 1122, according to the price at which it is meant to be sold. The general mode of charge is by the hogshead (about a barrel and a half), for which five pounds, six pounds, seven pounds, or eight pounds are paid, as the quality may warrant; the strength for every additional pound of price being increased by about four pounds per barrel of weight.

In a good fermentation, there seldom remains above a fourth of the original weight of the wort at the period of cleansing. Between that and a third is the usual attenuation. If above a third remains, the taste is generally mawkish, and it is to be feared that the acetous fermentation will commence, before the time in which the ale might be expected to improve. Of the less sensible process of attenuation which goes on afterwards in the casks, we have already spoken when treating generally of the "Vinous fermentation." Scotch ale soon becomes fine, and is seldom racked, at least for the home market.

We shall now transcribe the notes of a few actual brewings, in order to illustrate the rules above written.

No. 47.   MARCH 10th, 18—.   MASHED FOR STRONG ALE

13 *Bolls (about* 10 *quarters) of Malt*, T. L.*—42 *lbs. Hops, East Kent.*

Hour.	Min.		Bar.	Heat.	Grav.	7 o'clock Worts in Coolers.
						18½ Barrels X. Gravity 36 = 666
6	—	Mash	17	190°	—	6 ——— T. ——— 10 = 60
9	—	Set tap	—	—	36	10) 726
9	30	Sparge	1	180	35	Lbs. weight extracted per quarter 72.6
10	—	do.	1	180	34.2	
10	20	do.	1	180	35.2	*Fermentation.*
10	45	do.	1	176	35.6	Mar. 11. M. 5. Pitched at 50°. Yeast 3 Gals.
11	10	do.	1	178	35	Heat. Gravity.
11	35	do.	1	178	34	Mar. 12 50° 36
12	—	do.	1	175	35.7	15 52 33
12	20	do.	1	175	32.6	16 54 30
12	45	do.	1	174	27.5	17 56 26
1	10	do.	1	173	25	18 58 23
1	40	All in Copper.				19 60 20
						20 62 17
		Mashed for Table Beer.				21 63 15
						22 62 13½
			8	160		23 62 11½
						24 61 10½
2	20	Set tap.	8	—	7	25 61 10
4	10	Cast Copper, Ale.				26 60 9½ cleansed
						with salt and flour.

---

* The initial letters of the Maltster's name.

No. 49.　MARCH 16th, 18—.　STRONG ALE.

13 *Bolls (about 10 quarters) Malt*, T. L.—44 *lbs. Hops, Farnham and Kent.*

Hour	Min.		Bar.	Heat.	Grav.	8 o'clock Worts in Coolers.
5	—	Mash	16	185°		17 Barrels X. Gravity 40 = 680
8	—	Set tap	—	—	36.5	7 ——— T. ——— 11　　77
8	20	Sparge	1	180	36	
8	50	do.	1	180	36.5	10) 757
9	10	do.	1	178	37	Lbs. weight extracted per quarter 75.7
9	30	do.	1	175	37.5	*Fermentation.*
9	50	do.	1	175	37	Mar. 17. M. 5. Pitched at 46° with 3½ gal. yst.
10	15	do.	1	173	34	Heat.　　Gravity.
10	35	do.	1	173	33.5	18　　48°　　36
11	—	do.	1	172	30	20　　51　　32
11	20	do.	1	173	26	22　　53　　30
11	40	do.	1	172	26	23　　54　　28
12	15	All in Copper.				24　　56　　26
		Mashed for T.				25　　56½　　24
			8½	158		26　　57½　　20
						27　　60　　18
						28　　61　　16
						29　　62　　14½
						30　　62　　13
12	58	Set tap	8½		9	31　　61　　12
3	15	Cast Copper, Ale.				Apr. 1　　60　　11.7 cleansed.

No. 50.　MARCH 23rd, 18—.　STRONG ALE.

12 *Quarters English Malt*, E. G.—58 *lbs. East Kent Hops.*

Hour.	Min.		Bar.	Heat.	Grav.	March 24, morning, 4 Worts in Tun.
6	10	Mash	18	180°	—	20¼ Barrels X. Gravity 42.5 = 860.6
9	—	Set tap	—	—	44½	20 Barrels *Return*, Grav. 6.1 = 122
9	25	Sparge	3	180	44	12) 982.6
10	—	do.	2	180	42	lbs. weight extracted per quarter 81.8
10	35	do.	2	179	40	
11	40	do.	2	180	36	*Fermentation.*
11	45	do.	2	175	30	Mar. 24 M. 4 pitched at 51°　Yeast 4 Gals.
12	15	do.	2	175	25	Heat.　Gravity.
12	45	do.	2	175	20	Mar. 25　52°　41
1	5	do.	1	170	12½	28　56　39
1	20	All in Copper.				30　60　34
		Mashed for a Return.				Apr. 1　62　32
						4　65　29 added 1 lb. yeast.
			20	160	4	5　66　25
						6　67　23
						7　67　20
						8　66　18
4	25	Cast Copper Ale.				9　66　15
4	40	Return into Copper along with the Hops.				10　64　14.5 cleansed.

It may be observed, with respect to the left-hand portion of these tabular statements, that the *gravities* are taken as *averages* to direct the brewer in the number of his sparges, and are not minutely correct. The weights are those of worts, warm as they issue from the mash-tun; and, even in those small *sparges*, it would make some difference if taken from the former or the latter part of each running. The sparges themselves, too, may not be made with extreme nicety with regard to the quantity. The whole of the process, however, is easily acquired by practice, without which, in the manipulations of the arts, science is of little avail.

CHAPTER IX.

OF SCOTCH TWOPENNY.

AT and previous to the beginning of the eighteenth century, every publican in Scotland (being every man who chose to embark in the trade) brewed his own ale; and the resort to his house depended on the quality of his liquor; which, when thunder or witchcraft did not interfere, was generally excellent. The strong ale was reserved for holidays and the tables of the great; but the *twopenny* (so called because it was sold at twopence the Scotch pint*) was so much esteemed as a national beverage, that it was inserted by name, and guarded by peculiar privileges, in one of the Articles of the Union. Another Article, however, in the same Act, secured to the Scottish brewery an Exchequer Court; and this, conjoined with the enormously increased malt duties, so lessened the exhilarating qualities of this ancient ale, that it has now lost its fame. In its stead, a kind of small drink is brewed; but it is destitute of all the qualities which were so often celebrated in Scottish song, and is scarcely superior to the trash termed *table-beer* in the workhouses of the metropolis.

When the Scotch twopenny was the boast of the nation, saccharometers were unknown, and thermometers had not been heard of by the brewer. He shaped his course by habit, and with surprising accuracy, as blind men are often known to do. When we first knew the article it had much degenerated; but even then it must have weighed from fourteen to sixteen pounds per barrel, as far as we could judge from the lengths which they drew. The quantity of hops seldom exceeded two pounds and a-half to the boll of malt, or about three pounds to a quarter. This was forty years ago, and the old tapsters were then accustomed to tell tales of how they managed to brew ale without hops in their youth.

The boiled worts were usually cast into what were then called half-barrel casks, for few had coolers*; and the gyle-tun (which was often the mash-tun also) was first started, or pitched, at about blood heat. This was done with a single half barrel, or less, for the purpose of *chipping* the worts; and the tun was afterwards filled up, by half-barrels at a time, when they had cooled to the requisite degree. The heat of the fermentation was regulated by the appearance of the yeasty head, and great care was taken that it should neither be scalded nor chilled. When the smell of the tun became strong, the ale was cleansed into half-barrels, and discharged its yeast into tubs. But the whole brewing was never so fermented; for a great part, often one half, was preserved (in the casks in which it had been thrown from the copper) in the state of worts.

On reading this account of turning the worts boiling hot into the casks, and allowing them to remain there for several days, the modern brewer will immediately exclaim that the ale must have been *foxed*, a term which he gives to an incipient stage of putrefaction, which is supposed to be attended with a smell like that of the animal whose name it bears. We can assure him, however, that this accident was very rare, although it would probably be an inevitable consequence of the same practice in many other breweries. The great preventive was cleanliness. The casks were repeatedly washed and steamed with hot water before every brewing; and, in order that not a speck of dirt should be left, the bungholes were cut square, and large enough to allow the brewer to put in his arm, and scour them completely with a *heather rinse*. The large size of the holes, as well as the highly fermenting state of the liquor, rendered it inconvenient to use corks; and, therefore, when the ale was sent

* The *old* ale pint was nearly two English quarts.

* They held about sixteen English ale gallons.

out in casks, it was kept in the barrels by means of covers made of clay. "It is in allusion to this practice that Shakspeare speaks of tracing the dust of Alexander till it be found stopping a bunghole." *

After that part of the ale which was cleansed had discharged the greater portion of its yeast, a pailfull was drawn from every cask, into other casks, and the vacancy in each was replaced by a pailfull of the reserved wort. The fermentation was thereby renewed, and the operation was repeated once a day until all the reserved worts were expended; and those were so proportioned as to keep the fermentation *alive* until the succeeding brewing. This operation was called *handling*; and it was in this slowly fermenting state that the ale was sent out to the customers, in casks, or sold in flaggons. We have seen ale preserved, by this means, for nearly a fortnight, in summer weather, without the least perceptible tendency to acidity. Ale, in Scotland, whether strong or weak, was always bottled. In the kind of which we now speak, the cask was allowed to be undisturbed, before drawing off, for twenty-four hours, or perhaps twice that period, according to the length of time which it was to remain in the bottles before ripening. It was generally expected to be very brisk in the course of a week.

With respect to unlawful ingredients, we have already said that the Scotch are less to be complained of than their brethren of the South. The legislature, however, has, it seems, always thought otherwise; for, in addition to the caveats which are addressed to the whole island, there are some which are peculiarly directed against the brewers of Scotland. The following extraordinary prohibition, for example, is still in the Statute Book, and is regularly promulgated under the authority of the Excise:—

In Scotland.—By the Act Will., Parl. 1. Sess. 6. c. 43. no salt shall be made use of in brewing beer or ale, whether in washing and seasoning of vessels, or any other way whatever, under pain of confiscation of looms and vessels, with the liquor found therein, attour the loss of his freedom, if the transgressor be a burgess, and the being incapable to use the trade of brewing thereafter. The looms and vessels shall be given to the informer, who shall be free from the said penalty, albeit he have been a servant or accessory."

To prevent ale or beer from *foxing*, we are convinced that no cleansing material could be better than salt.

CHAPTER X.

OF BURTON ALE.

WE have formerly given Mr. Richardson's instructions for the brewing of this liquor; but we acknowledge that we have never been able to produce the flavour and permanent sweetness of Burton ale by following that gentleman's directions. The indiscriminate prohibitions of the Excise rise up before us, as they probably did before Mr. Richardson. They may have arrested his pen; but they shall not ours. We write not for the common brewer, but for the private gentleman, whose operations are unfettered. We will not say that the plan which we shall here point out is followed by the brewers at Burton, but we know that ale very like to theirs, in all respects, has been the result of this process.

Two ounces of salt of steel, dried until it becomes white, is infused into twenty barrels of liquor before mashing, that quantity of liquor being usually allowed for the first mash of ten quarters of malt. The use of this small portion of salt of steel is supposed to assist the extract; but we think that it has, more probably, been introduced to catch any incipient dose of oxygen which might favour the production of acidity. Its value may be questioned; but this small proportion, at any rate, is harmless.

Twenty barrels of this liquor is then turned upon the ten quarters of malt, in the ordinary way, upwards, through the false bottom. The heat is between 165° and 170°,—generally nearer the former. The mashing is continued about an hour, after which it is allowed to infuse about an hour and a half longer; the goods being covered with a sack of dry malt to preserve the heat.

When the first mash is run off, from ten to fifteen barrels of liquor (according to the proposed strength) is run over the goods at the heat of 185°. This

* Booth's Analytical Dictionary of the English Language.

is allowed to infuse two hours, when it will have sunk and mixed with the goods, without having been mashed. This differs from the Scotch practice by making up the length with one, in place of many sparges. Practice enables the brewer to fix the quantity of this second liquor; but he runs some risk of error in untried malts, while the Scotch brewer is always safe by weighing the wort in separate and successive portions.

This second liquor being run off, the strong ale worts are all extracted; and *table beer*, or a *return*, is made to exhaust the goods. It is usual, in the case of table beer, to cap the goods with a quantity of dry malt, which is understood to be necessary in order to procure the requisite strength. We believe that this practice (of which we do not approve) originated from a different cause. There was a time when the Excise objected to *party-gyles*, that is, to making two kinds of beer from the same malt; the *capping* was introduced to make (formally) a separate brewing, and was continued from the influence of custom. The least quantity of capping answered the purpose, so that it *covered* the goods, the strength being regulated by the quantity of liquor in the table-beer mash. This mash is generally made at 150° of heat, and allowed to stand about an hour:—but we return to the strong ale.

The quantity of hops is usually about six pounds to the quarter of malt, and the time of boiling from two to two and a half hours. From ten to fifteen minutes before turning off, a quantity of honey, at least equivalent to a pound per barrel, is put into the copper The honey is previously dissolved in scalding-hot liquor.

With respect to the fermentation, the tun is pitched at sixty-four or sixty-five degrees, with a pound of solid yeast per barrel. The first head is skimmed to rid the wort of the impurities which usually float upon the surface. After this the tun is generally kept covered, except when it is roused, which it is, twice or thrice a day. In from forty-eight to sixty hours it ought to rise to eighty degrees, or more; and when the gravity is about twelve pounds, it is usual to put half a gallon of bean flour and four ounces of sal prunella, previously well roused together in a portion of the worts, to every twenty barrels. The whole is then cleansed into barrels, which are filled up every two hours until they cease to discharge any yeast. Should the fermenting tun fall in heat, some recommend that two ounces and a half of jalap should be added for every twenty barrels of the wort.

Immediately after the casks have ceased working, six ounces of unburnt, but bruised, sulphate of lime, mixed up with an ounce of powdered black rosin, (both previously whisked in a small quantity of the ale,) are put into each barrel. Over this a small handful of half-boiled hops is also inserted; and the cask, being then quite full, is closely bunged up, having a gimlet hole, closed with a peg, at the side of the bung-hole, as an occasional vent for the escape of the carbonic acid which may afterwards be generated. The rosin and hops preclude the access of atmospheric air; and the sulphate of lime, which in a short time disappears, is said to prevent any secondary fermentation,—the usual forerunner of acidity. The honey is also understood to ward off the acid fermentation. Honey and water, especially when boiled, does not readily complete its attenuation, and hence it is supposed to answer all the preservative purposes of hops in the beer of Louvain.

The strength of the Burton, like that of every other species of ale, varies with the price. The qualities are seldom more than two; the one weighing from 30 to 32 pounds per barrel, and the other somewhere between 35 and 40, differing in the several brewhouses and with the demands of their customers. The latter, however, is accounted a *maximum* strength, and exceeded only in rare instances. Below 28 pounds the preservative quality, so peculiar to this sort of ale, is not to be depended on. The charge is usually by the gallon, because the sizes of their casks are various.

The following are notes of a brewing conducted according to the preceding directions :—

APRIL 27th, 18—.　MASHED FOR BURTON ALE.

Malt 6 quarters.—Hops 36lbs.—Honey 20lbs.—S. Steel 2oz.

Hour.	Min.		Bar. Liq.	Heat.	Bar. Wort.	Grav.	
7	—	Mashed.	12	165	—	—	April 28, M. 8. Worts in Tun.
10	—	Set tap.	—	—	—	—	12 Barrels X. Gravity 34.8 = 417.6
—	20	Spent.	—	—	7	35	10 Barrels Return in Copper,
		Run on.	9	180	—	—	Gravity 6.2 = 62
12	30	Set tap.	—	—	—	—	
—	50	Spent.	—	—	9	22	6) 479.6
1	—	In Copper.	—	—	16	27.7	Extract Gravity per Qr. = 79.9
·		Mashed for Return.	12	165	—	—	*Fermentation.*　Yeast 10 lb.
3	30	Mixed Honey.	—	—	—	—	April　28　Heat. 66　Gravity. 34.8
4	—	Cast Copper.	—	—	13	—	Morning 29　70　28
							——— 30　75　20
		Return and Hops in Copper.					Evening 10　80　14 cleansed.

In two days the ale had ceased throwing off yeast: and when it had stood two days more with occasional fillings, it was bunged up, after receiving a handful of half-spent hops, &c. as in the directions. This ale was kept through the summer; and, in the following September, it had become quite pure, and was bottled at a gravity of six pounds. In a month afterwards it became pretty ripe, and was well liked.

CHAPTER XI.

OF SMALL BREWINGS.

ALTHOUGH it is our wish that the Art of Brewing should be understood in every family of the kingdom, it, nevertheless, in its simplest form, requires manipulations that cannot be communicated in a few detached sentences, like the receipts of a cookery book. A certain degree of practice, however small, is necessary before general directions can be of any value; and, notwithstanding that we have endeavoured to be extremely plain, we fear that our observations would scarcely be understood by one who never saw a mash-tun, nor witnessed the production of a malt extract. It is, therefore, only to such as have already been present at private brewings, however well or ill conducted, that we are enabled to address ourselves; and to those persons we would recommend the attentive perusal of what we have already written, before they place their confidence in the succeeding examples.

For those families whose consumption requires, and whose means enable them, to brew two or three quarters at a time, our instructions may be simplified. Let them take any of the examples already given (according with the sort of beer, or ale, which they want) and diminish the measure of liquor in the mash, and the weight of the hops, as there specified, in proportion to the quantity of the malt which it is intended to brew. It would be well to keep to the same time of infusion; but, in that case, the heats of the mashing liquor should be four or five degrees higher; because, in small brewings, the mash-tun is apt to become so cool as to risk acidity in the worts. A like observation may be given respecting the fermentation. It must begin higher by five or six degrees; and it will be discovered, that under no circumstances will the heat of the tun rise so far above its first pitch as it usually does in large gyles. The criterion for cleansing and the previous proper attenuation to be aimed at are the same. In the case of porter, it will be more convenient to use pale malt, and give the colour (and consequent flavour) by means of sugar, burnt as directed at page 51. The aloes or quassia, which may be here used with impunity, will not only be a saving, but will be preferable to giving the whole of the bitter with hops.

In making strong ale, the private brewer is generally obliged to use more malt than he otherwise would; because, having no means of taking the advantage of a *Return*, he must make a quantity of small beer, whether it is wanted or not, for the purpose of searching the grains. In such a case, either the Scotch or the Burton system would be the best. His worts might thereby be made sufficiently strong without any loss of extract, and might be divided, as they passed from the tun, into any requisite strengths; either making the whole strong ale, or a part of it table beer, in such proportions as might be found convenient. The saccharometer would form the best assistant; and it would be extremely advantageous to quality and flavour, as well as to preservation, that the potency of the ale should be increased by the addition of honey. The quantity of this ingredient is to be regulated solely by taste; the mixture forming the link between *Malt Liquor* and *Mead*.

The history of the last-mentioned article is evidence of the baneful effects of the excise upon manufactures. The duties upon *Mead* were increased, from time to time, until it could no longer be made for sale. The duties, prohibitions, and penalties, still remain in the Statute Book; but we do not know that there now exists a single person liable to their inflictions. It is melancholy to see its expiring effort, in the excise accounts for 1808:—" The gross actual receipt in money" for duties on *Metheglin*, or *Mead*, during the whole year, is there stated to have been " one pound eleven shillings and six-pence." The quantity, on which this duty was charged, could not have exceeded twenty-one wine gallons; and the maker must have paid, besides, two pounds for a license. It might be supposed that these prohibitory duties, upon the manufacturer for sale, must be advantageous to private families who pay nothing; but in the present instance it is otherwise. Good mead cannot be brewed, even without duty, at less than five shillings a gallon, being equivalent to a shilling the wine bottle. It requires to be made in quantities of ten gallons at least, and is seldom fit for bottling in less time than a twelvemonth. With this outlay and care it once rivalled the wines of France, but the rich are contented with the latter, for which they are able to pay; while the poorer classes,

who, on occasional merry-makings, or in sickness, might prefer it to a bottle of adulterated port, can purchase it nowhere, and are unable to lay in a stock for themselves. This is one among a thousand greater instances of the price which the people pay for the wars they have been so fond of. Some directions for making *Mead* will be found in the *Treatise on Wine-making*, to which subject it more immediately belongs.

The midland counties of England have generally been famed for their malt liquors. That of Burton has already been particularly described; but those of Nottingham and Birmingham also find their way into the London market: indeed, any sort of country ale is preferred to what is usually manufactured, under that name, in the metropolis. Private brewing, too, is more general in the district above-mentioned, than in other quarters of the island; and the following description of the practice of a private family of our acquaintance in Worcestershire may be considered as generally prevalent in that and the neighbouring counties. It is obviously capable of improvement in regard to the saving of expense; but, in quality, the ale is by no means objectionable.

1. FOR GOOD COMMON ALE.

The strength of this ale was fixed to twelve gallons for every bushel of malt, and two bushels was the quantity usually brewed at a time; for which one and a half to two pounds of hops were allowed, according to their quality and the season. The Worcester hops were preferred as being milder in flavour than the Sussex or Kent. The malt was ground, rather coarsely, in which case it was supposed to drain better than when too fine; and the drainage was made to pass through a small cap-like wicker basket, called a *Betwel*, which was placed on the bottom of the tun so as to cover the entrance to the draining cock, or spiggot, as the case might be.

When every thing was prepared, and the liquor had begun to boil, the furnace door of the copper was thrown open, and the boiling having just ceased, as much of the hot liquor was run into the mash-tun as covered the bottom to the depth of an inch, or an inch and a half. About half a bushel of the malt was then put in, and stirred intimately with the liquor, until it was completely wetted. Another quantity of the hot water, sufficient to wet a second half bushel of the malt, was then let on; and this remainder of the first bushel was put into the tun, and the whole stirred together until every particle of the malt was supposed to be wet. The same process was carried on, by half a bushel at a time, mixed with continually added liquor, until the whole mash became completely soaked. A gallon of the liquor (as much as might have been contained within the draining basket or *betwel*) was then drawn off from the bottom of the tun, and thrown upon the top of the goods, which, after being covered with a sprinkling of dry malt, and *marked with a cross*, drawn over the surface with the end of the mashing oar, were allowed to rest, for the purpose of infusion.

When the mash had stood three hours, it was let off slowly into a tub (or underback) upon the hops, which had been previously steeped in hot water; and, after the draining was completed, an additional quantity of liquor (about the same heat as before) was laded regularly over the goods until the whole were as wet as at the first mash. This second infusion was allowed to stand an hour, when it was also run off, and transferred, along with the first worts and hops, into the copper for the purpose of being boiled. The quantity of worts required to produce the twenty-four gallons of ale (which, to allow for waste in boiling, might be about thirty gallons), was made up by sprinkling hot water over the goods, while the mash-tun was allowed to continue slowly draining.

When the worts had boiled in the copper for an hour, they were cast into wide tubs for the purpose of cooling. These being of different sizes, cooled unequally; but care was always taken not to mix hot worts with cold. A few quarts of the worts, when about milk warm, were stirred up with a quart of good fresh yeast, in the bottom of the fermenting tun, at which heat they rose into immediate action; and the remaining worts (except a small part) were added as soon as they were considered to be sufficiently cool.

When the head of the tun got very strong, and before it had begun to sink, the ale was cleansed; but previously to this being done, the bottom of each cask was covered about an inch deep, with the reserved worts above-mentioned;—we say the *bottom*, because the casks were placed upright, and discharged their superfluous yeast down the sides, from a wide tap-hole in the upper end.

In two or three days the fermentation generally subsided, so as to allow them to be loosely bunged; and in about a week more, after inserting a handful of half boiled hops in each cask, and filling it up, it was bunged up close, having a vent-hole and peg to loosen if necessary. In four months the ale was judged ready for tapping, and was drunk from the cask without bottling. This sort of ale is brewed, of course, at such times, and in such quantities, as to ensure a regular succession of four or five months old, keeping in view that the spring and autumn are the best seasons.

2. For Strong Ale.

The quality of the strong ale is calculated from the *length* that is drawn from the bushel. Some gentlemen make it a rule that a gallon of malt shall produce a gallon of ale; while others draw only five or six gallons from the bushel. The brewing of which we have now to speak consisted of twelve bushels, and from this about seventy gallons of strong ale were made. For this purpose about eighty gallons of wort were drawn from the goods, in the same manner as in the common ale. The hops (twelve pounds) were boiled with the worts an hour, or an hour and a quarter; and about the middle of that period *a lump of salt* (perhaps a pound) was thrown into the copper. Salt is also put, by some, in the common ale, in the same manner.

During this time, as much liquor was infusing with the goods as produced, when boiled and fermented, eighteen gallons of *very good* table beer. The hops of the strong ale were more than sufficient for the small, and part was usually kept out.

The fermentation was begun and conducted in the same way as in the last article, only with a larger portion of yeast, on account of the greater strength of the worts. The time in the fermenting tun was longer, the cleansing being guided by the appearance of the head, as it began to thicken. In cleansing, there was no reserved wort used, as in the preceding brewing.

In about three weeks after cleansing, the ale was racked into other casks; and a quart of ground malt tied in a clean linen bag was put into each. A handful of half boiled hops was also put in, and the bung made firm. Some persons put horse beans, either bruised or whole, in place of the malt, and also a few egg shells and a pound of loaf ·

sugar to a barrel, with the view of better preservation.

This ale was kept six months in the cask before it was tapped. It was then bottled, and ran no further risk of acidity, although kept for years. October or November is accounted the best season for brewing, because the six winter months are understood to be most favourable to the keeping of ale that is newly brewed. When it has passed those months, it runs less risk of acidity during the succeeding summer, in the case of its continuing in the casks.

On reviewing the preceding directions, it will be observed that much is left to the experience of the brewer, which, from the want of instruments, cannot be communicated to the reader. The heat of the mashing liquor was probably above 190°, but this is left to conjecture. It must have varied with the heat of the atmosphere, but in the worst direction; for, in cold weather, the liquor would be at a lower when it ought to be at a higher temperature. The heat of the fermentation must have been liable to the same accidents. The proper period for cleansing, too, must have been very difficult to ascertain, there being no mode of discovering the attenuation; and in consequence, under such management, the strong ale might be ready for bottling two or three months sooner, or it might be protracted two or three months later than the period intended.

The mode of mashing (akin to the Scotch *sparging* system) is capable of drawing out the whole strength of the malt, were it not for two prominent errors: one of which is the consequence of the other. The want of a false bottom makes coarse grinding necessary to enable the worts to work their way to the basket. Without either fine grinding, or crushing, the malt cannot be sufficiently searched; and, unless the sparges are allowed to descend in horizontal strata, we leave one side of the mash-tun to be less acted upon than the other. We are well convinced that, in the fore-mentioned examples, and especially in the second, one-third of the extractible saccharum of the malt was left in the grains.

In the details of which we now speak, the reader's attention was particularly directed to the *cross* that was drawn on the surface of the goods. This *sign of the cross*, in those counties, is universal, although no one knows why. The

Protestants consider it as a remnant of Popish superstition. There is, however, no superstition in the case. It is a useful proof of the perfection of the process. After the mashing is finished, and the goods strewed over with dry malt, the cross can only be fairly drawn when the whole of the goods are completely broken. If any knots or lumps remain, being lighter than the rest, they rise to the surface; and meeting the rod by which the cross is drawn, they will break the continuity of the line. A similar practice is observed by the maltsters in Scotland, and perhaps in other places. After a floor has been turned, the maltman makes *a cross* on a corner of the surface with the end of a shovel, the appearance of which shows whether the grains of the malt be well separated, or clotted together. Formerly, every craft had its mysteries, which were hid from the uninitiated, for whom some wonderful tale was invented that might satisfy their curiosity without adding to their information. Another of those mystical symbols will be seen in the following instructions, which were sent to a lady by an eminent Scotch brewer:

" *Leith*, 11th *November*, 1793.
" DEAR MADAM,
" * * * I have sent you 18 lbs. of hops. I generally put in 7 lbs. to the boll* of my best ale, but I think 6 lbs. of these hops should do; and, as good store (yeast) is essentially necessary to the making of strong ale, I have sent you up as much in a small cask as will answer your brewing, the produce of my double ale.
" * * * * * I shall use the freedom of mentioning a few directions, at least, that I follow:—I, in the first place, allow the liquor, or water, in the copper, to come to a boil for ten minutes or so. I then run it off into the mash-tun, and cool it to 190 degrees by the thermometer: or, if you have not one, you may stir it for eight or ten minutes, which brings it near about it. I then put in the malt, and stir it well till all is wet. I then throw a little dry malt, which is left on purpose, on the top of the mash, with a handful of salt, *to keep the witches from it*, and then cover it up. I allow it then to stand three hours, and then let go the cock of the mash-tun, and run off the wort slowly, to keep it fine, into the wort-

---

* About 9 lb. per quarter.

stane*. When the frst is run off, I sparge it with liquor at 180 degrees; allowing the cock to run all the time till I have as much as I want of quantity. I then pump the worts into the copper, (having put more liquor on the goods for the following, or small beer, at 160 or 165°) and allow them to boil *for an hour.* Having mashed the hops with liquor at the time of sparging the malt, they are put in when putting the worts into the copper. After they are boiled the *above-mentioned time,* I throw them (the worts) into the coolers, and allow them to stand till cool. I then let them into the tun, giving them some store; and, after they are *chipped*†, I add more store by degrees; and, mixing them frequently with a scoop, or cudy‡, I let them stand still till the fermentation is very strong; perhaps three days. I then tun (cleanse) them into casks, filling up twice, or thrice, a day till properly wrought.   *   *   *

> "I remain, with esteem, &c.
> "W. G."

Mr. G.'s directions, though less minute than those of our Worcestershire friend, show a little more of science, by the introduction of the thermometer. It is surprising, however, considering the comparatively recent period at which he wrote, and his fame as a brewer (for he was the first of his day), that he makes no mention of the saccharometer, in default of which, or something equivalent, no brewing, whether great or small, can be conducted with advantage. Without it, good ale may be made, but the expense, in family brewings, is not calculated: and the proverb is forgotten, that "what is the private gentleman's boast would be the public brewer's ruin." Further, what with some is reckoned a matter of more consequence, the quality is always uncertain. The malt, it may be, contains a less quantity of fermentable matter, or it does not give out the extract at the heat usually employed. In either case, the same length is drawn; and the discovery is made, a year or two afterwards, in consequence of the obvious weakness, or degeneracy, of the ale. There was a time when instruments were unknown in the brewery; but there was also a time when a *jug,* of indefinite dimensions, was taken as a measure; and a *stone* was selected, by guess-work, from a field, as a representative of weight. Those days, however, are gone by; and, with the degree of knowledge which we now possess, the expectation of being able to brew good malt liquor, without knowing the strength of the worts, seems almost as absurd as to attempt the process, without either weighing the hops or measuring the malt.

Additional information on this subject will be found in the pamphlet which accompanies "*The Brewer's Saccharometer,*" an instrument made and adjusted under the direction of the writer of this treatise.

_____

While closing the present treatise, we are well aware that we have left it imperfect. This is partly owing to the narrowness of the limits that have been assigned to it, which has obliged us to abridge many of the illustrations. The treatises on *Wine-making,* and the *Manufacture of Cyder and Perry* (which are, in fact, continuations of *Brewing*) will afford opportunities of remedying, in a great measure, these unavoidable defects.

---

* A stone underback.
† Creamed on the surface.
‡ A *Cudy,* or *Cuddy,* is a small shallow pail, having one of its staves lengthened and shaped so as to form a handle.

ERRATA.

Page 16, col. 2, line 4 from the bottom, for *qualities* read *quantities.*
Page 32, note, dele *last* and read 1829.

Made in United States
Orlando, FL
06 May 2022